The Wall of Champions, Bitsy Grant Tennis Center, Atlanta Georgia 2009

Photo by the author

TENNISTOWN USA

THE GOLDEN AGE OF GEORGIA TENNIS

STORIES OF THE PLAYERS
THE GEORGIA TENNIS HALL OF FAME
THE WALL OF CHAMPIONS

ROBERT ANTHONY RIVES

For my father, Davis Rives

All proceeds from the sale of this book in excess of actual publication costs go to "Friends of Bitsy," a non-profit organization dedicated to the preservation of Bitsy Grant Tennis Center in Atlanta, Georgia.

Tax deductible donations may be made by sending a check to Friends of Bitsy Grant Tennis, 1266 West Paces Ferry Road, Box 113, Atlanta, Georgia 30327; or by credit card online, http://www.bitsytennis.com/index.php/

COVER

Until 2011, the wall of the stairway going to the lower level at Bitsy Grant Tennis Center displayed photographs of Georgia tennis players from the early 20th century through the 1990's.

It was often referred to as the "Wall of Champions." On the upper level was the Georgia Tennis Hall of Fame, a separate room containing photographs, trophies and memorabilia. The Hall of Fame has now been relocated. Only a few of the pictures are still displayed.

contents

the players

contents

out-takes

*left over material that didn't quite
fit, but will be of interest to some readers*

ACKNOWLEDGMENTS

The project would not have been possible without the cooperation of many people. A few of them: Mary Grant MacDonald, Bitsy Grant's daughter, who not only devoted many hours in gathering together family photographs, but drove from her home in Newberry, SC several times to meet with me and share memories about her father and the Grant family; Dan Magill, who made available the Collegiate Tennis Hall of Fame photos, and granted permission for use of excerpts from his two books, and shared his photographic memory of events and players going back many years;

Beverly Shields, who spent hours studying disintegrating scrapbooks at the Bitsy Grant Tennis Center to determine names and dates; Harry Thompson, who graciously loaned his personal collection of clippings, photos and memorabilia, including an original copy of *"The History of ALTA;"*, Richard Howell, who made the Howell family scrapbooks available for study and copying; Ellen Johnston, Librarian of the Georgia State University Library, for researching the Atlanta Journal-Constitution archives held there;

William and Mary College, for helping me contact alumna Donna Floyd Fales, who then entrusted family photos to the mail for scanning and for spending time talking numerous times about her father and uncle, and their early involvement in tennis in Atlanta; Donna's cousin Mary Collins, who shared photos of her father and uncle, and took time to meet with me several times to supply information and stories; Joe Becknell, both a gifted player and a talented writer, who shared stories and anecdotes in his unique style; Charlie Cox, the founding father of ALTA's mammoth league operation, who loaned his personal collection of photos and recollections of the early days of the Atlanta Lawn Tennis Association; J. Larry Jones, for his colorful recollection of long ago meetings with Natalie Cohen, having nothing at all to do with tennis, but descriptive of Natalie's willingness to help any one in need;

The Jack Browdy family, for sharing Jack's many photos; my Marist (high school) doubles partner J. Donnely Smith, whose tennis life touched many of the players on the "Wall of Champions" and in the Georgia Tennis Hall of Fame, for sharing his memories of them; Martha Kelly, Sonny Mullis' niece and keeper of his memorabilia, for sharing it with me; Gene Asher, for granting permission for use of images and text from his *"Legends-Georgians Who Lived Impossible Dreams;"* Judge Marvin Arrington, for granting permission for use of excerpts and photos from his *"Making My Mark;"*

The Georgia Tennis Hall of Fame and Bitsy Grant Tennis Association for preserving and guarding many photos over many years; John Callen, Ron Cioffi, the USTA/Southern and the Southern Tennis Association, for sharing images and information from their wonderful book, *"Southern Tennis;* Barbara Howell, without whose enthusiasm and unflagging support I would never have started and certainly never have finished the project; my now deceased tennis companion Ken Woods, for patiently listening to my concerns about the destiny of photos and the history behind them; my soul mate of 57 years, Florence, for many hours of proof reading;

And finally my late father Davis Rives, whose enthusiasm and support I could feel all the way.

FOREWORD

Readers may wonder how this work came about.

A few years back, one of our Bitsy Grant Tennis Association board members, the late Ken Woods, mentioned that a friend of his was concerned about preserving all the pictures on the "wall of champions" and in the Hall of Fame. It didn't seem important. The pictures on the wall had just been re-done a year ago, and so we saw no reason to get involved, our pictures were just fine, and we had bigger things to talk about.

A year later it came up again, this time from another board member, who reported that Ken's friend had pointed out that there were more than a few pictures on the wall that no one recognized, much less knew anything about. A few on the board knew Ken's friend casually; his father, Davis Rives, had been involved fifty some years ago with ALTA as a board member and president, and had been a regular player at Bisty, knew all the older players, and this was his son. He wanted to copy all the pictures and the plaques. We finally voted to give it a shot to see what he would come up with, hoping he wouldn't hurt any of our pictures, and there was no cost involved. I was probably the one most positive about it, because of my long association with the Atlanta History Center, and my fascination with the idea of preserving the past.

For a while we heard nothing.

We had some scrapbooks of events at the center, mostly social and fundraising things, and he borrowed those for copying. They had been kept at the center for years, and as it is with most scrapbooks, they were shuffled around, stuffed in drawers, dropped from time to time, put into corners, and were in general disrepair, pictures falling out here and there, many without identification nor date.

In 2009 we were planning a gala fundraiser, and it seemed like a good idea, now that we had a digital record of the pictures, to put some of them together in a booklet and try to sell them. He did it. They didn't sell well enough to make any real money, but it showed us what the possibilities were. As it progressed, it began to appear that at some point, there might be some kind of publication of what he was working on, and so as not to leave out any of the many people involved in tennis in and around Georgia, we decided to involve other people. We formed an advisory group, of both amateurs and professionals, the Georgia Tennis Association, the Georgia Tennis Foundation, the Atlanta Lawn Tennis Association, and our own Friends of Bitsy. A record of the history of the sport of tennis in Georgia would be nice.

Barbara Howell

PREFACE

For years I would get sidetracked when I walked down the stairs to the locker room at Bitsy Grant Tennis Center, looking at the pictures hanging on the wall. I knew most of them, and began to think they might some day be gone, the pictures themselves and certainly the information about who was in them. I wanted to do something to preserve what was there.

Along the road in pursuit of theses objectives, a lot of trails ran off in different directions. After a few phone calls, stories emerged. Some of the calls produced humorous twists. Laura Henry, Crawford's daughter, called me, only after my sending an old fashioned snail mail paper letter with stamp attached, my last resort when the phone calls and emails failed. Turns out I had signed the letter "Tony." Her dad , when she first told him their phone caller ID said "Robert Rives" had called, had said, "*...I don't know anybody by that name…*" Their telephone "mailbox" was full, so I hadn't been able to leave a message. He knew a Tony, but not a Robert.

Another one went: "*...Allen, this is Tony…*" '*Who?*' "*Tony Rives*" - - - '*...well, OK, now, how do I know you?*' "*Well, Allen, think back about 60 years. We both played some at the Atlanta Tennis Club, and some at Northside, and we rode together with a bunch of other kids a few times to Athens to play in the GIAA, and one time you were sitting next to me in the back seat of somebody's car, and offered me a sip from your Budweiser, which I took; and you said, '...damn, don't kill it!!!…'* And you knew my Dad; he used to tell me not to try to hit the ball "*like Allen, he hits it so hard that a lot of them go out...*" And on and on.   '*....Oh, yea, its coming back to me now…*'

In an hour long phone conversation with Donna Floyd Fales, whom I had not seen in over 60 years, I was amazed that she remembered Sunday afternoons at our house on Clifton Road. A few minutes, and it seemed like only yesterday.

Readers will find some inconsistencies; some individuals are included who have never been on the "Wall of Champions" nor in the Georgia Tennis Hall of Fame, but whose stories seemed in concert with the spirit of the work. Conversely, some players who are on the "Wall" and/or in the Georgia Tennis Hall of Fame have not been included because information was not available, and in a few cases because the individuals themselves were unresponsive and seemed to have minimal interest.

The geographical parameter was initially the state of Georgia, but as research progressed it became obvious that information on people, tournaments and tennis events outside Atlanta was in short supply. My apologies to those communities, many of whom have very active and thriving tennis communities.

All personal recollections, as opposed to third party information developed through research, are in a separate box, in quotation marks and italics, followed by the name of the person being quoted, except my own, which are identified as "*Author.*" The word "Bitsy" is used both as a reference to the man and the place named for him. Hopefully the context will make clear to readers which is intended. The word "Kalamazoo" is used frequently, with no explanation. The reference is to the most significant tournament for junior boys in the world, the USTA National Championships, from the 12's through the 18's, which have been held at Stowe Stadium on the campus of Kalamazoo College in Kalamazoo, MI since 1943, open only to highly ranked juniors.

INTRODUCTION

I remember going to the Atlanta City Auditorium back in the early 1950's, to see the Jack Kramer tour. By today's standards, it was a small crowd. I got in free, serving as one of the linesmen, and we had the best seats in the house. I was inexperienced, so they put me on the service line. Once the ball was in play, I could sit back and watch without concentrating on calling a line. I remember being particularly awed by how Pancho Segura managed that long, graceful, sweeping two hander off both sides. And I got to shake hands with Tony Trabert, what a great guy. Pancho Gonzales was the polar opposite, socially. He vehemently objected to one of my calls, not challenging the call to the chair, but walking over and getting in my face. He said, *"...I can see why you wear glasses!..."* But the call stood. On reflection, I think it was for show, and I was the fall guy.

There was of course no tennis court in the City Auditorium; it was mostly a place for wrestling matches, dances, and concerts. The Kramer group carried with them a huge heavy canvas surface, in two sections, which they stretched tight, with lines imprinted, and a portable net. They sold tickets; I can't remember the cost, but it wasn't much. And it wasn't a "tournament" so much as an exhibition, like the Harlem Globetrotters, except they weren't from Harlem and it wasn't basketball. Kramer played Gonzales a set; Segura played Trabert; Rosewall played Riggs, and so on, and you really couldn't tell how serious they were about winning. A lot was showmanship, playing to the crowd.

It was a one night stand. They were gone the next day, I was unaware of just how good they all were. I hadn't followed Kramer's spectacular Davis Cup record just a few short years back, and had no idea of his personal financial struggle to make it in the game, like working in a meat packing plant (owned by Wilson) to make ends meet, and selling the family car in 1946 to finance wife Gloria's trip to Europe to watch him play.

The focus of the work is preservation of the history of the era, people in the sport in Georgia from its beginnings through the 20th century, an era that was largely "amateur," an age whose heroes were not in it for the money, who were largely self taught, who had to put bread on the table with a day job,. They played because they loved it. The Kramer entourage were not amateurs, but they might have well been because by today's standards they made very little.

The transformation of tennis into "open" was not without disagreement. Many felt the introduction of money would destroy its purity. Ironically, the evolution of tennis as a major spectator professional sport has resulted in far more amateur participation than had it never happened.

Tennis today is a different time in history, adequately chronicled in the media. Hence, if not much is found in these pages about it's current heroes, it's because there is not much more to tell.

Robert Anthony Rives, 2011

TENNISTOWN USA

IS IT IN THE WATER?

Mention Atlanta to any tennis buff whose job has taken him to there, and you're likely to hear, *"Oh yea, we played ALTA, it was great…"* For almost 40 years now, Atlanta has been the envy of players everywhere in the country for its addiction to tennis.

Forty years ago it was like a lot of US cities of 500,000 more or less, a good place to live and work, and OK for tennis with 10 or so public facilities and a half dozen private clubs. Then the city grew. Ten fold, now around 5,000,000, with a reasonably temperate climate that allows one to play tennis all year, unlike northern cities where it's spring, summer and fall, with frozen courts in the winter.

But by far, the biggest factor in the tennis explosion in Atlanta was Charlie Cox' brainchild and the meeting in 1971 at the Squire Inn on Piedmont Road. He had had discussions with teaching pro Ruth Lay about the successful "interclub" meets Lay had organized between private clubs. Could the same thing be done on a larger scale? If so, players could be charged a modest fee for organization, the proceeds going to ALTA to help it achieve its mission of staging tournaments. Support for the idea among the ALTA board members was not unanimous, but fortunately those in favor prevailed, and the rest is history. Cox conceived and personally typed up rules a few days after the meeting, and had them "*mimeographed*"[1] for distribution. By summer's end, an obscure organization with a few dozen members had become 2000, and a bank account of a few hundred dollars soared to over $10,000.

The original format, with its simple classification of A, B, and C players has endured, albeit with a few tweaks to accommodate the explosive growth, make play competitive, and prevent "sandbagging." There are now levels AA, A, B, and C, and within each level, up to 9 flights, with end of season playoffs and finals. Initially there were both singles and doubles; singles matches have now been virtually eliminated, disappointing many serious tournament players, many of whom enjoy singles.

The explosive growth was not without problems. Court availability on play days became tedious for those not in the league loop. Formation and entry of a team now requires two courts available for matches. As complications arose, they were solved by an ever growing list of rules.

BITSY GRANT TENNIS ASSOCIATION

On June 4 1975, the Cumberland Indoor team took first place in the ALTA spring league play after a clutch playoff match. Bottom row, L-R, Bobbie Hall, Eleanor Swann, JoAnna Kennard, Merrie Ann Park, and Beverly Shields (Capt.). Top, Jo Ann Snavely, Ellen Katz, Barbara Tregellas, Nancy Falkenburg, Leah Froshin, Julie Wrege, and Sally Haas.

---

[1] *Mimeography used a crude hand-cranked machine to duplicate documents before the age of electronic photocopying.*

BAG TAGS, TOURNAMENTS, ANOTHER LEAGUE, AND PLAYER RATING

BAGTAGS

Photo by the author

In the 1990's, almost ten years into ALTA[1] league play, the idea of plastic tags being given as trophies was hatched, and proved instantly popular. They became a badge of honor, showing the world that one was a winner. The more successful a player was, the more tags there were, and the rattle of bunches of them dangling from tennis bags, clattering as the team walked on court, was intimidating, and said, *"here come some tough players."* It was a stroke of genius. Other types of trophies have been tried, but none have ever been as popular as the tags.

1996 saw the U.S. Women's' Hard-court Championships staged at the Olympic Tennis venue at Stone Mountain, Ga., featuring Lindsay Davenport, Monica Seles, and Jana Novotna. Others, including Martina Navratilova, Billie Jean King, Pam Shriver, Rosie Casals and Tracy Austin were part of the lineup for a Legends of Tennis Classic that would be the opening act for the tournament. Unfortunately attendance was embarrassing, and the tournament moved to anther city the next year.

In 1998 the Nuveen Champions Tour played at the Atlanta Athletic Club, featuring such greats as Matts Vilander, Mikael Pernfors, John Lloyd, Jimmy Connors, and others. Again, fans disappointed. Atlanta seemed more interested in playing than in watching.

In 1998, a Davis Cup match between the U.S. and Russia came to Atlanta, and this time the fans did not disappoint.

Success is hard to hide. In 1978, the Southern Tennis Association (perhaps inspired by ALTA's runaway popularity) lobbied the USTA to launch a pilot program of league play, starting with four communities, (none in Atlanta), and pulled equipment manufacturer Penn into the loop to furnish the balls. The USTA concept was to rank competitors according to skill level determined by something called a "League Evaluation Placement Questionnaire." It was intended to identify a player as falling into one of the seven categories used, and was the forerunner of the "National Tennis Rating Program", aka NTRP. It was perhaps thought that the simplicity of the ALTA A-B-C system would not work on a national scale. Thankfully this system has been greatly simplified, now describing 7.0 as being "...a world class player…" down to 1.0, described as "this player has never played a set of tennis."

---

[1] *The origin of the acronym was from the "Atlanta Lawn Tennis Association," a mouthful. The initials were easier to handle in conversation, and at first, the letters themselves were pronounced, individually, and the organization was referred to early on as "the A.L.T.A." The periods after the letters have now been dropped and it's become a word, pronounced phonetically. Though there are no (known) genuine grass courts in Georgia now, the connection with the "lawn" courts of the past remains. The USTA, formerly the "United States Lawn Tennis Association" dropped the word long ago.*

A TEACHING PRO BONANZA,
COURTSIDE BUFFETS, TENNIS BRACELETS,
AND DESIGNER CLOTHES

One might think, with 50 states to draw from, rather than from a single city, USTA league play might have by now eclipsed ALTA in size and left it behind as an anachronism, a dying star in the tennis cosmos. What's actually happened is that the USTA operation in all 50 states is roughly 325,000 (in 2010), not the millions one would expect. One can only conclude that Atlanta is a special tennis place.

In the days before Cox and ALTA, there were "teaching pros," but the idea of a group of amateurs having a "coach" was unheard of.

Now, a team without a coach is like a ship without a rudder. The quest for winning became a driving force. Casual weekend players, women particularly, discovered that teaching pros could help win bagtags. Initially coaching was allowed during matches, until it was stopped. But coaching during practice is now regarded as a necessity if a team wants an edge.

League match
buffet spread

Another byproduct of league play in Atlanta was the discovery of the social side. People are brought together that would never have mixed without the camaraderie of a team. Some drive Bentleys, others arrive in old pickups.

At one time, no one would have thought to bring food to a tennis court, unless it were a paper bag with a sandwich, and a coke. Nowadays, courtside buffets provided by the host team are a matter of pride, and run the gamut from store bought nibbles on paper plates to foie gras and wine on china.

Then along came the "tennis bracelet." Some credit Chris Evert with its origin. She was known for her line of diamond bracelets that she wore on court, and the stopping of her match in the 1987 U.S. Open to let her search for one that came off during play, still known as the "tennis bracelet incident," was a dream come true for jewelers everywhere, popularizing the thin bracelets with diamonds that she wore.

BUNY GRANT TENNIS ASSOCIATION

Blackburn Tennis Center's 1991 USTA 4.5 team, after winning the finals of the Georgia Championship against Columbus, Ga. at the Jekyll Island Tennis Center.

BITSY GRANT
TENNIS CENTER

A SPECIAL PLACE

Named after Georgia's icon of the game, it's deceptively ordinary. There are no gates, guard houses, valet parking, initiation fees, applications for membership, dues, no grand stone buildings with ivy covered walls, no dining room, nothing to mark it as special other than the number of courts, 23, the largest facility in the city when it was built. What makes it very different, however, is its core of hard working dedicated volunteers, working through two non-profits, "Friends of Bitsy" and the Bitsy Grant Tennis Association, who have saved it many times from slipping into oblivion.

The latest lifeline was thrown in 2009 when it was obvious that the cash-strapped City of Atlanta could not do much more than keep the lights on for the foreseeable future. The volunteer organizations came up with half the $1,000,000 price tag for a much needed major renovation, completed in July 2011

Celebrities are frequently seen there. Columnist Lewis Grizzard was a member of the "Tree Bar Club," which would congregate for libations under a tree on the front lawn. Former Tech head basketball coach Bobby Cremins has played there, as has former Mayor Sam Massell. Janet Jackson came by one afternoon a while back to hit a few balls. Legendary Georgia football coach Bobby Dodd was a regular for years. Michael Childs, former nude dance club owner (and nephew of former Atlanta mayor Andrew Young), is back among the regulars after a stint in federal prison. A CNN anchor plays there, as does a certain Creative Loafing senior editor. It became the place for action during the tennis boom in the city.

Some say it brought the game out of the elitist country clubs and made it available for folks who couldn't otherwise afford to play.

"It's a little community here," says regular Ernie Garrison. *"Everybody knows everybody. You'll have a group of people congregating on the porch and games just developing out of the blue. It's the only place I've ever seen where you can do that."*

But special it was, and is. Since its construction in the early 1950's and until the present day, it has been a mecca, a gathering place for Atlanta's best players. Usually one would expect to find exceptionally talented players dispersed, geographically, rather than concentrated in one venue. But at "Bitsy" they are often seen together on any given day of the week and at any time, either playing, watching, or talking, some coming every day of the week.

And with them have come the foot soldiers of the game, some serious but limited in ability, some with more than average skills, and some more socially motivated than dedicated to improvement.

A few have been coming for more than 50 years, others only a short time, and some come and go, but all are immediately members of and accepted by the group. On its veranda, overlooking court one, one almost always sees players watching, talking, kibitzing. *"Hey, wanna play? We got a court in 15 minutes and we need a fourth..."*

The last half century has been a golden age for Bitsy Grant Tennis Center. Recently a returning player, away for a long time, upon walking up and seeing Grant, Crawford, Bird, and Dodd on court one, was heard to say, *"look out there... the only place in the world where time stands still..."*

RALPH FOSTER

COURTESY BITSY GRANT TENNIS ASSOCIATION

If any one person epitomizes the spirit, the essence, the joie de vivre of Bitsy Grant Tennis Center, it would be Ralph. Never a player ("*I don't have time to learn*"), he presided over the operation for over 30 years with humor, guile and mischief, but with silent and skillful efficiency. He got the job sideways, so to speak; he had applied to the city to be a fireman, but found he was afraid of heights, and the Bitsy job just happened to be open.

In retrospect, his engaging personality and savoir faire would have opened many doors, particularly anything involving people. He could mix with anyone regardless of social level. He aced the job. He was much more than a "manager." His presence and style created an atmosphere of conviviality that would do credit to a state department ambassador.

Checkers were another passion. He was a skilful player, and often complained about having "jumper's cramps."

One of his amusements was using the loudspeaker system as his personal toy. A notable example, oft repeated around the center to this day, was once when he sensed that teaching pro Joe Becknell might be trying to impress a comely young thing while giving her a lesson on one of the far courts. Ralph seized the opportunity, and announced loudly over the PA system, "*Joe, your wife called—she says be sure and pick up the baby food on your way home…*"

He had a penchant for nicknames, and had one for everybody (that he liked). Names like "Who-Two", "Midnight", "Slow Foot", "Turbo", "Beep-beep", and countless others.

One notorious incident was conning Bitsy into a bet on a horse race in the Kentucky Derby that had already been run. As the story goes, Ralph and 10 or so buddies are downstairs watching a horserace on TV. They record it, and when Bitsy comes down the stairs a few minutes after it finishes, Ralph says, "*Hey Bits, we've got the TV on a race that's about to start; I'll take no 4 in the 5th, against the field.*" Bitsy, sensing a sure thing, replied, "*you're nuts, but you're on for $5.*" They hit "play," the fourth race recording starts, and they all cheer No. 4 across the finish line. No one knows for sure, but its most likely Ralph did not keep the $5.

TOTAL PRIZE MONEY $3500 !!!!

NOTE WELL - All rounds must be played by the designated time or the most culpable team will be immediately DISADAMNQUALIFIED. First round to be played by July 31st. Second by August 14th. Third by August 24th. Fourth by September 5th. Finals and gala victory celebration will be Saturday, September 13th.....details later.

NOTE WELL #2 - All players must notify their purchasers if they intend to buy a portion of their team by midnight (EDT), July 18th, or before their first match, whichever is sooner. If they have not notified purchaser, it is assumed they will not purchase.

THE CHOLLY CUP

Any description of Bitsy Grant Tennis Center would be incomplete without mention of one of its most popular activities. Shortly after construction of the center, an imaginative and innovative player, Charlie Ellis, conjured up one of the most successful tennis activities ever seen anywhere. He coined it the "Cholly Cup." It became an immensely popular summer mixed doubles tournament running over several months each year, with its own Calcutta betting system, prize money and tournament rules, with heavy recruiting in the Peachtree Hills singles community. Unsanctioned by USTA but nobody cared. It racked up a 25 year run, interrupted only by Charlie's decision to move back to Savannah. The stained bulletin board notice above was retrieved from someone's scrapbook of ancient photographs. An impatient Charlie was obviously exhorting participants to play assigned matches on time, or else.

Charlie Ellis, beer in hand, laying out the rules (and laying down the law) to Cholly Cup participants,

THE TREE BAR

Another fixture of the center was given its name by noted columnist, author and raconteur Lewis Grizzard. Its center of operation was the area around a magnificent white oak in front of the center close to the driveway, away from the hustle and bustle of the "porch," and its "bar stools" (concrete benches) surrounded it. Sadly, the great tree succumbed to a thunderstorm in 1991, and was replaced, courtesy of Trees Atlanta, with a number of young saplings, one of which was planted in the exact spot of the old matriarch. In the great tree's heyday, lawn chairs and coolers were there, providing shelter from the summer heat, when the porch was full, solace from defeats, elation from wins, and a convivial atmosphere for the many tall tales being related under her comforting branches. Many half-truths and more than a few outright lies filled the air, sometimes intermixed with spellbinding orations, embellishments, and perhaps some genuine hallucinations, stimulated by various libations, from such notable barroom experts as Grizzard, *("Shoot Low Boys, They're Ridin' Shetland Ponies", "Does a Wild Bear Chip In The Woods",* and others). Despite all the gossip and lies she heard, the old girl silently kept it all to herself, never tattling. She gave up, like many old tennis players, after being weakened by old age and disease, mercifully euthanized by a sudden rain storm, never revealing her secrets. The Tree Bar lives on.

See also p. 122

TOURNAMENTS GALORE

Atlanta has hosted many tournaments from early on. The Atlanta Invitational began in the early 1900's.

As time went on and the popularity of the game increased, events became more innovative. One such was the Saks Fifth Avenue Mixed Doubles "Kodel" promotion in 1975. In Atlanta and other cites around the country they played in shopping center parking lots. The one in Atlanta was at Phipps Plaza, near the Saks store. The winners of that first event , played at the Grossinger's Resort in New York, were a Houston teaching pro and her partner, an IBM employee. They got a free entry into the U S Open that year.

In the '70's and '80's, Lamar Hunt's[1] Peachtree World of Tennis hosted many pro events. It closed in 1990 after almost 13 years. The Atlanta location became Racket Club of the South.

The Atlanta Pro Invitational, the Prudential-Bache, the AT&T Challenge, and the Nabisco Grand Prix were all going on in this period, some at the Omni, some at the Tech Coliseum, and some at Dunwoody Country Club. It was a busy time for professional events in Georgia.

In 1996, wheelchair tennis was an event in the Olympics at the Stone Mountain Tennis Center, constructed especially for the event, over the objections of the Georgia Tennis and Atlanta Lawn Tennis Associations, who both wanted another location. It was a beautiful facility. In the wrong place.

PICTURES COURTESY BITSY GRANT TENNIS ASSOCIATION

1961 Atlanta Invitational Tournament, court one, a beautiful fall day at Bitsy Grant Tennis Center

1975 Saks Kodel tournament Atlanta, at Terminus Tennis Center; Ned Neely and partner Joanne Snavely, left, Atlanta qualifier winners over Lewis Smith and Pam Engel, right. Neely and Snavely advanced to the finals in New York City.

COURTESY STADIUM ATLAS

Stone Mountain Tennis Center, Dekalb County Georgia

[1] *Sports promoter Lamar Hunt is credited with putting pro tennis on television, before the days of the International Tennis Federation and the ATP. The facility in Norcross, Georgia was one of several built around the country.*

THE CRACKERLAND TOURNAMENT

The first of Dan Magill's many sports promotions was his personally starting the Crackerland Tournament while a student at the University of Georgia. It enjoyed a remarkable run of over 50 years, and there is likely no serious player in the state who reached success in the last fifty years who did not play in it. As a result, their paths crossed with Magill's along the way, and he remembers them all, not just their names, but details about their lives.

"It doesn't seem like it was 61 years ago when the Crackerland tournament started. It was the summer of 1939, and I had just finished my freshman year at UGA and had begun my summertime job of managing the University's six old red courts in front of LeConte Hall...the annual Athens City and Northeast Georgia championships had been held on these courts since they were built in the mid-30s, and I was eager to put on a tournament that might someday be considered a "big" one." The Georgia State tournament was locked-in by Atlanta, and the Southern championships rotated to only the largest cities in the South. My father, then editor of The Athens Banner-Herald, actually gave it a good name: the Crackerland, which was a respected and well-known cognomen in Dixie and especially Georgia.

"The second year, 1940, we succeeded in attracting some of the South's best players, headed by top-ranked Lou Faquin of Memphis, Tenn., who defeated Atlanta star Cortez Suttles in a hard-fought match, 6-2, 6-4, 6-4. A highlight of the finals was the presentation of a gigantic silver-plated trophy to champion Faquin by Athens' Mayor Bob McWhorter, Georgia's first All-American football player in 1913.

"University of Georgia officials were pleased that we had a junior division in Crackerland, and they permitted the juniors to stay free in dorms on the campus, hoping some of them would enroll at Georgia. It was during the "Depression Years" and there were very few students at the University.

"I came back to Athens in the summer of 1950, after spending WWII in the Marines and then 3 years in Atlanta as a sports writer for the Atlanta Journal/Constitution, and resumed the tournament... it gradually grew into one of the South's most popular sectional tournaments through 1995, before it ended when I retired from UGA...

"Some of the best players in the history of U.S. tennis have played in the Crackerland. Its graduates have won an amazing total of 191 USTA national men's tournaments (all age divisions) and 22 in women's divisions... I'll never forget Allen Miller of Tucker and Lisa Spain of Moultrie when they made their Crackerland debuts. They were so young that their parents "baby-sat" them..."

Dan Magill, "Oral History of the University of Georgia," 2000

COURTESY HARRY THOMPSON

Crackerland junior players between matches, UGA varsity courts, Athens, Ga., 1959

2010 NCAA Mens' finals,
Henry Feild Stadium, Dan Magill Complex, University of Georgia

Photo by the author

Words cannot describe the atmosphere when a University of Georgia team reaches the NCAA Division I finals when they are played in Athens Georgia. Tennis has a reputation for gentility and reserve; it goes out the window when Georgia plays a match on its home courts in the Dan Magill tennis complex at Henry Feild Stadium, with fans cheering every point, not just those won but all of them. Visiting tennis teams are intimidated and unnerved because of the sport's traditional reserve and politeness. It's no wonder many NCAA tennis coaches objected to UGA's frequent hosting of the championships, given the 13 year consecutive run in Athens from '77 to '89.

Hopkins Indoor Courts, UGA

Photo by the author

The complex had humble beginnings. In 1900 the university built its first courts at what is now the intersection of Broad and Jackson streets. The present site has 16 courts (12 outdoor and four indoor) and a total seating capacity of more than 5,000 fans. It is one of the largest on-campus tennis facilities in the country.

OLEG CASSINI AT THE UNIVERSITY OF GEORGIA

COURTESY COLLEGIATE TENNIS HALL OF FAME

1936 was a down year for UGA tennis; they went 1-6 for the season, defeating only Wayne University.

But an upside that year was a foreign player, one Oleg Cassini-Loiewski, the freewheeling, charming globe trotting European who would later become famous for designing clothes for first lady Jackie Kennedy in the salad days of her husbands presidency.

1936 University of Georgia tennis team, L-R, Captain Wade Hoyt, Ed Sutherland. Plott Brice, Treville Lawrence, Ed Landau, Albert Jones, Aaron Cohn,

and Oleg Cassini

Cassini came from high to low to high. He was born in Paris of Russian and Italian aristocracy, and grew up there and in St. Petersburg. His father served the Czar as Secretary of the Russian Embassy in France.

His immigration to the U.S. was on a shoestring; legend has it that he arrived with $25, a dinner jacket, and a tennis racket. Poverty was a new experience. As a child, he had learned fencing, skiing, piano, horsemanship, English, and tennis. His family's fortunes slipped after the Russian revolution, so to get a fresh start, they adopted his mother's Italian surname and relocated to Florence, where his mother opened a dress shop, Maison de Couture, and began successfully rebuilding the family finances.

When Oleg immigrated to the US, he found tennis to be a door opener; he played in clubs and tournaments up and down the East Coast for "bed and breakfast" (presumably maintaining his amateur status by taking no more than expense reimbursement). His stint at UGA must have been brief, perhaps only one year. The picture above, which hangs in the Collegiate Tennis Hall of Fame museum, appears to be a composite, constructed from individual images. Possibly the "1938" on two jerseys represents the year of graduation.

Exactly how he got into this picture is unknown, but there he is. Team member Aaron Cohn, still working, (a sitting judge at age 97), confirmed to UGA Coach Emeritus Dan Magill in a phone conversation in January 2010 that Cassini had been ineligible, but did in fact work out with the team that year. He became a US citizen, and served in the US Calvary during WWII. Cassini reputedly competed at Wimbledon, the U.S. Championships (before the Open era), the French Open and Davis Cup. Oleg's interest in tennis continued throughout his life. His second wife, actress Gene Tierney, complained in divorce proceedings in 1953 that her husband valued his tennis more than her. He led a colorful life, marrying three times, but never allowed vows to distract him from pursuing beautiful women.

THE UNIVERSITY OF GEORGIA
AND CELEBRITY DOUBLES

A public appearance by a celebrity is a sure fire formula for boosting attendance at almost any event. Putting them on a tennis court with professional players is even better, and was adopted in 1983 by Dan Magill as an adjunct to hosting the NCAA tennis tournament, in an effort to increase ticket sales. It quickly became a popular event, featuring well known names playing with and against professionals. Magill's feeling was that the audience was titillated by the possibility that one of the celebs might "*mess up*" (sic) during a match. Surprisingly, none ever really did, and many gave credible performances.

Kenny Rogers' formal education was limited, and he was self-taught musically. But according to Magill he was a quick learner, and "*...was just a natural athlete. He could have been good at anything. He never picked up a racket until he was well past 40, but learned quickly. He got pretty good...*"

Singer/song writer/actor Kenny Rogers, above, with pro partner Dennis Ralston.

Rogers put down roots in Athens after marrying fourth wife Marianne Gordon, an actress and native Athenian, and set about building Beaverdam Farms, on 800+ acres of rolling land near Athens, with amenities fit for royalty, including an equestrian facility and an 18 hole golf course. Sadly, the marriage did not endure, and Kenny "folded 'em" and moved on. But his legacy in Athens is alive and well in the building he made possible with a generous gift, the Intercollegiate Tennis Association Hall of Fame.

Heisman Trophy winner Herschel Walker played with Dennis Ralston in the 1986 Celebrity Doubles. Magill remembers asking Herschel to play; and hearing, "*...let me think about it, Coach...*" A few days later, he replied positively, "*on one condition*". What's that, Herschel? "*Well, you gotta teach me how to play...*" So arrangements were made for the coaching staff to pull out all the stops to make him competent in the 14 days remaining before show time. He was a quick study, often returning to the varsity courts later after coaching, to "work out" with friends. Magill, in his daily scrutiny of goings on around the complex, noticed some strange black marks, almost like tire tracks when a car skids, on the otherwise pristine surface of court one. Asking James Payne, his longtime assistant, about the marks, he heard, "*...well, Coach, the only person I know whose been down there much besides the team has been Herschel...*" Turns out the "Goal Line Stalker" had no tennis shoes, and was playing in basketball shoes. That deficiency quickly then remedied, his tennis boot camp continued, and Herschel was transformed by the coaching staff almost overnight into a tennis sensation. He and Ralston prevailed.

COURTESY COLLEGIATE TENNIS HALL OF FAME

Football star (UGA, NFL, Heisman winner) Herschel Junior Walker,
with pro partner Dennis Ralston in the 1986 Celebrity Doubles

*"Lewis Grizzard was fond of observing that he was
the only person from Moreland who ever made the
New York Times best seller list. And the only person
in Moreland who ever heard of the New York Times.*

*He once wrote, "Life   I do love that word." And
live he did. Four wives, 450 newspapers syndica-
tions, millions of fans, hundreds of appearances, and
oceans of vodka.*

*"I remember another occasion, many yeas ago in the
stands of Sanford Stadium in Athens, Ga., for the
annual Georgia-Georgia Tech game, during one of
those extremely rare moments of silence at a football
game, I (and everybody within fifty feet) heard the
sound of ice clinking into a glass. Grizzard, sitting
two rows down from me, was recharging his drink.
His female companion was shushing him. He kept
clinking.*

*"We met numerous times, but he never remembered
who I was. When I would jokingly say, "how're
things in Moreland?" he would most often say,
"...you from Mo'land?"*

*"Moreland, Ga., Grizzard's birthplace, is Georgia's
Mayberry, a small town just south of Newnan. He
was a pretty fair player."*

Author

COURTESY COLLEGIATE TENNIS HALL OF FAME

Top ten tennis legend Ham Richardson, left,
with partner USTA President Randy Greg-
son; they defeated author and humorist
Lewis Grizzard and pro Tut Bartzen in the
1985 Celebrity Doubles

COURTESY COLLEGIATE TENNIS HALL OF FAME

Hall of Fame Curator Magill with tennis writer/commentator Bud Collins in 1983, shortly after the opening of the building.

THE COLLEGIATE TENNIS HALL OF FAME UNIVERSITY OF GEORGIA CAMPUS ATHENS, GEORGIA

The Intercollegiate Tennis Association (ITA) selected the University of Georgia as the site of its Collegiate Tennis Hall of Fame and Dan Magill as chairman of the Hall of Fame Committee and Curator of the Hall of Fame museum in 1982.

In 1983, the first members were selected, and inducted in ceremonies during the 1984 NCAA Championships in Athens. The project was made possible due to the generosity of the Rogers family (Athenian Marianne and her famous husband, singer Kenny), who handled the entire cost. The Hall of Fame inducts members annually, honoring past collegiate players, coaches and contributors dating back to 1883 when the first national tournament was held, making tennis the oldest national collegiate championship.

Visitors can view a collection of images and memorabilia, assembled single-handedly by Dan Magill, consisting of more than 800 photographs and large news clippings featuring Hall of Fame members, NCAA singles, doubles and team champions, winners of ITA's national tournaments, collegians who have excelled in Davis Cup play, Grand Slam winners, and UGA players going back to the late 19th century. There are numerous racquets used by champions from different eras, including replicas of the 90-year-old ones used by the first U.S. Davis Cup team players in 1900, and the first tennis rulebook in the country (1879). Private donations fund the Hall of Fame operations including the upkeep and improvement of the numerous displays.

Dan Magill on the funding of the Collegiate Tennis Hall of Fame:

"... They put the Collegiate Tennis Hall of Fame here because we were putting on the NCAA championships. We drew the biggest crowds. They put the Hall of Fame here, and I was trying to raise money for the Hall of Fame building. That was back in 1983. That was about the time Kenny Rogers married the beautiful Mary Ann Gordon of Athens. He had met her on the set of 'Hee Haw', a TV show. She was one of the pretty girls, never did say anything, just looked pretty. She...you remember Nurse Goodbody on that show? She wasn't Nurse Goodbody, but she could have been. They moved to Athens. She had helped me in her high school days. She had helped me because her grandmother was the bookkeeper in the athletic department, and Mary Ann would come down there to visit her grandmother, and her grandmother called me and said 'Mary Ann's getting in the way, I can't balance the books. Put her to work.' So I paid her 50 cents an hour helping in my office, folding envelopes, before they had folding machines, and licking stamps before we had a stamp machine.

> "Turned out to be the best investment I ever made. When she and Kenny were married, he built that palace out there near Colbert, Georgia (Beaverdam Farms), and he had taken up tennis. She brought him down here and wanted to know if he could play tennis on our courts. I said, 'Sure.' Then shortly thereafter, he said he wanted to make a financial donation to the tennis program. I said, 'We're trying to get money for the Hall of Fame.' Well, he ended up paying the whole amount, $200,000. He never finished high school, never went to college, and never took part in any sports, but he was a natural athlete. and of course he was a great singer and made a lot of money out of it. We benefited by it. Originally, I put a bronze plaque in front of the building that said, 'Thank you, Kenny Rogers, for your generosity to college tennis.' He said 'Take that sign down.' I said, 'You're the boss.' I took it down. He said, 'Now put another one up there and say 'Thank you Mary Ann and Kenny Rogers.' That's the sign we have up there now, a bronze plaque."

ORIGIN OF THE TENNIS TIEBREAKER

Lower right, Dan Magill with James Van Alen, at Van Alen's induction into the Collegiate Tennis Hall of Fame in 1984. Most league and tournament players today are familiar with the "12 point tie-breaker," first player to reach 7 points by a margin of 2 winning the set. Very few know the history of this tiebreak device, invented by Van Alen in 1965, and its journey through many variations.

The first was known as the VASSS (Van Alen Streamlined Scoring System), first used in the US Pro Championships in 1955 and 1956. It was a table tennis like thing, first to 21 winning the set, and no second serve. The theory was to speed up play, and limit the effectiveness of a big server, the biggest of the day being Pancho Gonzales. Speed up it did; in 1955, Gonzales defeated the other Pancho of the day, Chilean two hander Segura, in 5 sets by a slim margin, 21-19, and it took only 47 minutes. Fans disliked it, and in 1957, scoring returned to the traditional format.

In 1969, an epic struggle pitting Gonzales this time against Charlie Pasarell went 5 sets, games totaling 112, took 5 hours 12 minutes and stretched over two days. In 1971 Wimbledon introduced the tiebreaker in sets reaching 8-all, with the 5th being played out. Most tournaments today have some variation of this protocol. No doubt the influence of television and advertising, not to mention court time in amateur matches, have had a lot to do with shaping the tie-breaking convention.

Van Alen was of noble heritage, a descendant of two wealthy American families, the Astors and Vanderbilts, whose summer "cottages" were in Newport, RI, where he grew up. He was educated at Cambridge, where he played on the tennis team, and while there he became an expert at the game of Kings, court tennis. He became world champion in this obscure version of what we play today. He passed away in 1991 at age 88.

COURTESY COLLEGIATE TENNIS HALL OF FAME

Magill with Van Alen, 1983

Bill Moore Tennis Center

Photo by the author

The Bill Moore Tennis Center at Tech today is a long way from the old clay courts in Peters Park. The center was constructed in 1988, largely through the efforts of letterman Bill Moore, for whom it is named. There are 12 outdoor and 3 indoor courts, with lighting and seating that make it an ideal venue for collegiate play.

One of Tech's most memorable seasons was 1960, when they won the SEC title with a comeback from nowhere. On the last day, the Jackets had to have a clean sweep, win all five of the last five matches. And they were facing teams to whom they had lost. They astounded everyone when they pulled it off. Ned Neely won at number one singles by defeating Tulane's Crawford Henry, 8-6, 6-0. Harry Thompson also won, at number 2 singles; then he and Neely won at number one doubles; Metz won at number five singles. Then Dave Peake and Dave Pearsall at number two doubles clinched the title for Tech by a two-point margin over first-seeded Tulane. The Jackets finished the season with a 10-8 record, and gained their first SEC title in 18 years, the third for Tennis Coach Earle Bortell. Rounding out a beautiful season, Neely and Thompson traveled to California for the NCAA doubles championships, and reached the finals. Thompson set a personal record for his play from 1954-1960 that still stands, 64-11, .853. Neely's record for the same period was .769. Bob Nichols' 1959 record was .828, Walter Johnson was .818 for '64-'66, and Kenny Thorne during 1985-1988 was .717, but has the most career wins (all matches), 112.

> *"At practice, Coach Bortell indulged his fondness for cigars. The rumor was that he kept an apple core in his pocket with the cigar, to keep it moist. He always came straight from class, and was covered with blackboard chalk. My 1951 team was not spectacular; we had some good players (all better than me) but nothing like the teams that followed, when Bortell got a tidal wave of talent, a lot of it coming from the Jack Waters' training ground at Westminster."*
>
> *Author*

Tech's victorious 1960 SEC championship team; top row L-R Ned Neely, David Peake, Jerry Averbuch, Coach Bortell; bottom row L-R Harry Thompson, Paul Metz, and David Pearsall.

Bitsy Grant's brother Berry played at Tech in the '20's. A 1927 *TECHNIQUE* article observes:

"Captain Grant issues first call for tennis practice. The Tech tennis team will begin practice Monday afternoon...

"Due to bad weather, practice has been delayed, but several courts have been worked and put in condition for the practices which get under way next week. Prospects for another championship team are bright with such notable stars as Captain Grant...and Pee Wee Merry, Scotty Morton, Walter James, Wright Widegood, Walter Merkle and Jim Lewis.

"In the conference tournament Berry Grant and Pee Wee Merry won the doubles and although Tom Slade of Florida won the singles title the Jackets were given the conference championship due to the splendid record made during the season...

The annual conference tournament will be held at Chapel Hill, May 13 and 14. At present the team is scheduled to journey to Philadelphia to enter the National Intercollegiate Tournament."

One of Tech's most successful coaches of all time is the current (2011) Womens coach, Brian Shelton. His teams have won 70 percent of their matches, making him the winningest tennis coach in Tech history.

His players include 10 All-America selections and 20 All-Atlantic Coast Conference players in nine years, nine Academic All-America or All-District honorees, 49 student athletes named to ACC Honor Roll (3.0 GPA or higher), and a school No. 1 national ranking during 2006 and 2007 seasons, and a No. 1 final national ranking in 2007.

Quite a few honors have come Shelton's way: the 2007 USTA/ITA National Coach of the Year, the 2002, 2005, 2007, and 2008 ACC Coach of the Year, the 2005 and 2006 ITA South Region Coach of the Year, a 1993 Georgia Tech Hall of Fame Induction, a 2002 Georgia Tennis Hall of Fame Induction, and in 2006, a Huntsville-Madison County Hall of Fame Induction.

BIGHOUSE TENNIS

PLAYING ON THE RED CLAY AT THE ATLANTA FEDERAL PEN
MCDONOUGH BLVD, SOUTHEAST ATLANTA

Back in the 1970's, the warden, Fred T. Wilkinson, a tennis player who occasionally showed up at Bitsy Grant Tennis Center, began a custom of inviting visitors into the prison to play against the inmates.

They had two red clay courts, immaculate, in exactly the right state of dampness, regularly being watered, brushed, and rolled There was a grassy hill on the side of one of the courts, convenient for spectators; on another side was a wall of concrete that looked to be 50 feet high, with guard lookout towers.

The courts were extremely popular with inmates. They stayed busy during the daylight hours, on a "king-of-the-hill" rule; the winner of a match stayed on the court, and the next challenger came out and played him.

There was always a long queue to play the winner. Surprisingly, they all had what appeared to be decent rackets and shoes. Sometimes a ball would fly over the concrete wall, and almost in unison, players and spectators alike would shout, "...*I'll go get it!*" Always predictable.

1966, an Atlanta team playing at the Atlanta Federal Pen. L-R Buzzy Cowart, Don Smith, Sonny Mullis, Miles McGowan, Arthur Howell, Dan Hankinson, and Bob Nichols. Whether the big smiles are for a win, or for just getting out of the place is unknown.

"Usually four of us would drive there, go through a security process, and then through a series of sliding iron gates, inmates everywhere giving us curious looks because with our rackets and tennis clothes on we were standing out like sore thumbs. That 'clank' when one gate closed behind us before the next one opened in front of us was always disconcerting. No one was saying 'Hi' or rushing over to shake hands.

" The inmates are walking around doing their thing, in various stages of undress, but you could tell you were being watched. We were clearly out of our element.

"One curious aspect to the adventure was that none of the inmates used anything other than a first name, usually a nickname. I played a singles match against 'Cool Breeze.' All I remember was that he had holes in his shoes and ran like a jackrabbit, running down and returning everything. He was closed-mouthed about why he was there, changing the subject when a question was asked.

"I remember only one who talked at all about his situation. He was 'Ramon,' and explained that he was there on a drug charge. He had been a Brazilian Air Force pilot, and it seems some controlled substances had found their way into hidden spaces in his fighter plane and discovered when he landed in Miami. He explained that he had no idea how they got there. He must have been upper class in Brazil, because his English, with only a slight accent, was perfect and his tennis strokes were smooth and polished, the kind one learns with coaching, perhaps at some private club in Rio. He was matter-of-fact, resigned to doing his time, affable, not bitter, and interesting to talk to.

COURTESY BETSY GRANT TENNIS ASSOCIATION

"*Oh, don't worry, we'll get you out...*"

Sonny Mullis playing at the
Atlanta Federal Pen, 1962

"On one of our trips, after playing, one of our inmate/opponents cordially invited us to stay and watch the afternoon movie. 'It's a good one,' he exclaimed, excitedly. I expressed some concern about our pass expiring, and the guards expecting us to leave right after playing, and what might be involved in explaining to them that we had stayed to watch a movie. 'Oh, don't worry, we'll get you out...'

I did worry.

And I didn't stay for the movie.

Author

Fred Wilkinson later became national director of the Federal Prison system. His philosophy throughout his career was rehabilitation, not punishment. Now long retired, he stills works (in 2011) for this cause.

James "Whitey" Bulger served three years in Atlanta in the mid-1950s for armed robbery and hijacking before heading a crime ring that controlled much of the narcotics trade throughout New England. Old-school Mafia Don Vito Genovese ended up in Atlanta for heroin dealing not long after he had finished bumping off rivals to secure his place as boss of the country's pre-eminent crime family. Reportedly, he continued to run the family business from behind bars in Atlanta until his death in 1969. Another notable resident was Vincent Papa, a major New York drug runner. In 1957 Rudolph Abel, a Soviet superspy, moved in.

Al Capone landed in Atlanta in 1932. Two years later, federal authorities shipped off him to Alcatraz. He spent his remaining years dying of syphilis.

Another semi-home grown inmate was Atlanta baseball star Denny McLain. He had finished his career with the Atlanta Braves, and was suspended for running a bookmaking operation. He once had his toes broken by a Mob loan shark, and was later convicted of racketeering, extortion and cocaine possession. McLain called Atlanta the filthiest and most dangerous of the many prisons he'd known, once writing: "*After Atlanta, the men's room at a Texaco would look like a hospital operating room.*"

In 1956, the Federal Pen's tennis representative Jack Wolfe wrote Sonny Mullis, right, expressing sadness that he didn't make the finals in the Georgia State Open, and that all the inmate/players were pulling for him.

"*Sometime in the 1970's, an Atlanta boy, Mike Thevis, became a resident of the Atlanta Federal Pen. He was briefly held there before being sent off to another federal prison, in Minnesota, to serve a life sentence.*

"*I remember him from when he attended Marist when I did, in the 50's, and had been an altar boy at Sacred Heart Church, as I was.*

"*I never saw him with any friends. He worked afternoons at his family's newsstand on Broad St. I don't recall his ever saying two words, just sitting on a little stool amidst the girlie magazines and newspapers, in front of the cash register, more or less expressionless. A few years after graduation, I read about his arrest in the paper.*"

Author

THE EARLY DAYS

The popularity of the game was divided in the early 20th century between "lawn tennis," a social diversion for the well-to-do who could afford a court in the backyard, and the serious pursuit of tournament play. The later had its roots in the late 19th century. The U.S. Men's Singles Championship was first held in 1881 in Newport, Rhode Island. The Orange Lawn Tennis Club, in Orange NJ, hosted the US Championships in 1886. In 1898, The Atlanta Athletic Club constructed two courts at it's "country club," known as East Lake. The site of the courts is now a parking lot for the "East Lake Golf Club," which has no connection with the Athletic Club. The International Lawn Tennis Federation came up with standardized rules in 1924, rules that have remained remarkably the same to this day.

COURTESY GEORGIA ARCHIVES, VANISHING GEORGIA COLLECTION, IMAGE NO. CAM 195

Nancy Carnegie and friends on a lawn tennis court, on her family's estate on Cumberland Island, Georgia[1], ca 1920, posing in a somewhat Gatsbyesque fashion, perhaps between garden parties, swimming, walking on the beach, lawn bowling, and other diverse activities. She was married there in 1920 to James Rockefeller, and shortly afterward the grand mansion was abandoned.

[1] *The Carnegie family bought he island for a winter retreat in the 1880's and constructed a 59 room mansion called Dungeness, modeled after a Scottish castle. It was surrounded by pools, a golf course, and 40 outbuildings to house the 200 servants who worked there. Later, additional estates were built for Carnegie children, including Greyfield, now a private inn, Plum Orchard, now maintained by the National Park Service, and Stafford Plantation, now abandoned. Dungeness burned in 1959. It's ruins remain at the south end of the island. The family sold their land to the National Park Service in 1972.*

PLACES LONG FORGOTTEN

In Atlanta in the 1930's there were few public courts. Those at Piedmont Park, Grant Park, and Candler Park still survive. Peters Park, the dream of developer Richard Peters, became surrounded by the Ga. Tech campus. The four there were for years the home courts of the Ga. Tech tennis team. Buildings now rest on the site. There were also some private but open to the public courts such as the Northside Tennis Club on North Avenue near Peachtree St., with its grandstands and lighting, the Atlanta Tennis Club on Argonne Ave., and the Biltmore Tennis Club at Peachtree and 4th St. All are now gone. The fifty or so members of the Atlanta Tennis Club "kept up" their natural red clay courts themselves, with regular watering, brushing and rolling. Their courts were surrounded with fencing of chicken wire, and the members paid dues of $5/month. Most of the members were serious tournament players, among them Malcolm Manley, Jack Teagle, Ralph Bridges, Nat Collins, Dr. Ralph Akin, and Donald Floyd (below, right, circled, serving as a linesman). The Northside Tennis Club was founded in the early 1920's by Doc Wilson, president of the Wilson Shirt Company.

COURTESY GEORGIA ARCHIVES, VANISHING GEORGIA COLLECTION, IMAGE NO. LUM212

The 1905 North Georgia Agricultural tennis team, Dahlonega, Georgia.

COURTESY GEORGIA ARCHIVES, VANISHING GEORGIA COLLECTION, IMAGE NO. JAC 007

A wagon near Commerce, Georgia, ca 1904, one passenger ready with racket should they pass a court on the journey.

Below and facing page, Wilmer Allison defeats Bitsy Grant before a large crowd in the 1936 Atlanta Invitational at the Biltmore Tennis Club, Atlanta, Georgia

COURTESY DONNA FLOYD FALES

Bryan Morel Grant
1909-1986

ATLANTA HISTORY CENTER

Bitsy Grant, ca 1940

Bitsy was born in Atlanta, Ga. On December 25, 1909 into a tennis playing family. His father, Bryan M. Grant Sr,[1] a prominent, successful businessman and sportsman, was a serious and accomplished tournament player and was the Southern doubles champion for many years. Bitsy's older brother Berry was captain of the tennis team at Georgia Institute of Technology in Atlanta. He was a member of the Piedmont Driving Club, as was his father before him.

Despite his size, Grant became a star in football, basketball and tennis at a young age, and attended the University of North Carolina, where he was named a tennis All American in 1931. He lead his team that year to an undefeated season. Rumor has it that he was on campus for over three months before the tennis coach, John Kenfield, even knew he was there. Near the end of his coaching career in 1955, however, recalling the years Bitsy played for him, Kenfield ranked Bitsy as the best he had ever coached. It was not all work and no play, however; the records show Bitsy pledged SAE fraternity.

In the years 1935 to 1937, Bitsy defeated in major tournaments many world class legends, including Don Budge, Frank Shields, and Wilmer Allison. He reached the quarters at Wimbledon in 1936 and 1937, losing to Fred Perry and Bunny Austin. In 1937, Grant and Wayne Sabin were the 3rd-ranked U.S. doubles team. He played Davis Cup in 1935, 1936, 1937 and 1938, helping the U.S. regain the prize in 1937 after a 10-year slump.

One of his few defeats that year was to Baron Gottfried von Cramm[3] of Germany, with Herman Goering watching, certainly never dreaming at the time that in just a few years he would serve in the U.S. military in a war against the country he was playing in.

He won the U.S. Championships (later known as the U.S. Open) on clay three times. He was also successful on the grass courts of Forest Hills, New York. He won 8 of 11 tournaments entered in 1935, and did not lose one match on clay courts. Some tennis analysts believe that Grant's retriever style of play was so draining that after a demanding match he had little energy for the next round. In 1933, a sports writer described him as "...*one part greyhound, one part marathon runner, and two parts mechanical man...*" He was most feared on clay, but privately confessed later in life that he really preferred faster surfaces.

His heritage is noteworthy. His great grandfather[2] came to Atlanta from Frankfort ME to work as a laborer on the Georgia Railroad. By 1844 he began buying large tracts of Atlanta real estate. He became a surveyor's assistant, and eventually an engineer. In 1852 he founded, with others, the Atlanta Bank, and in 1873 he organized the Bank of Georgia. Atlanta's Grant Park was established in 1882, as well as Westview Cemetary, when L. P. Grant gave the city of Atlanta 100 acres in the newly developed suburb where he lived. He died in 1893, a highly respected founding father of Atlanta, and was buried in Westview Cemetery.

---

[1]   *B. M. Grant Sr. held a USLTA national singles ranking in 1908 of no. 34; he was a runner-up (with Dr. Nat Thornton) in the U. S. Open Mens' Doubles in 1912; and was Southern Singles champion in 1913.*

[2]   *Lemuel P. Grant became president of the Georgia Railway in 1848, and president of the Southern Pacific RR in 1858. In 1856 he had built a three story Italianate mansion in what would later become Grant Park; the mansion was later the birthplace of Georgia's golf legend Robert Tyre Jones. It now houses the Atlanta Preservation Center.*

[3]   *Von Cramm was debonair, handsome, charming, and Nazi Germany's No. 1 player.*

B. M. Grant, Sr.
ca 1905

Bitsy was never a professional. At the height of his career, there were only a few professionals, and they were bared from amateur events. Had he come along 50 years later, he probably would not have spent 30 or so years selling insurance for the Cobb Torrance Agency in Atlanta.

He served in the Army Air Corp in the Pacific during WWII, where he contracted malaria, which caused him to retire briefly from competitive tennis after the war. He recovered fully.

The press covered his tournament play almost daily, particularly his Davis Cup matches. He became a celebrity, well known for his tennis triumphs, and was selected to escort another celebrity, movie actress Olivia de Havilland, to the December 13 1939 premier of "Gone With The Wind" at Atlanta's Loews Grand Theater. The film's stars stayed at the Georgian Terrace Hotel at Peachtree and Ponce de Leon Ave. after flying in to "Candler Field." He was 29 at the time.

Noticeably absent from the premiere were Hattie McDaniel (Mammy) and Butterfly McQueen (Prissy), black actresses with major roles whose presence as dignitaries would no doubt have caused great consternation in Atlanta's segregated society. A young Martin Luther King, Jr., however, was there, singing in a "negro boys choir" from his father's church, Ebenezer Baptist.

Once during "The Championships" at Wimbledon, the Queen expressed a desire to meet *"...the barefoot boy from America…"* After extensive coaching as to proper protocol, the meeting took place, and he greeted her as *"ma'am"* instead of as *"your majesty."* His southern upbringing had taught him to address elders as "sir" and "mam." It reportedly charmed the Queen.

The "barefoot" thing was a circulated rumor, referencing his having played on the grass at Wimbledon without shoes because he could not find grass court shoes small enough to fit his feet. No one knows for sure.

He was always at his best on clay, the surface he grew up on. At his peak, he was almost unbeatable on it. Ellsworth Vines once cut the strings out of his racket after going down to Bitsy on clay, and vowed never to play on clay again. Shortly afterward he was again vanquished by Bitsy, this time on grass, but didn't make the same promise about not ever playing on grass. He might have run out of surfaces and strings.

With little power and limited reach, Grant adopted a retriever style, running down every ball and keeping it in play as long as possible, which, combined with phenomenal ball control and excellent conditioning, made him difficult to beat.

He did not give in to age, and was able to reinvent his game as the years wore on, relying on angles, lobs, and drop shots, all executed like a magician, combined with his trademark demeanor on court, often feigning exhaustion, then coming to life to reach what appeared to be impossible gets. He won his 11th and final Southern singles championship in 1952 at the age of 41.

In 1956 Bitsy announced his plans to play in the U.S. Open in the open age division. He had just turned 46. The USTA had just implemented a policy of allowing only players under 45 to play. Discouraged, he then said he would not play at all. Friend Natalie Cohen pleaded with him to enter the senior division, and to convince him, she organized a luncheon, and invited many of his friends, all of whom had also agreed to play as seniors. He finally relented, and won the 45's on both grass and clay that year. Lucky for the open division players. He would probably have steamrolled quite a few of them.

Just a few years later he blew through a stunned Stan Smith (a former U.S. Open and Wimbledon winner), at the time many years his junior, in the Atlanta Invitational in 1958.

Grant liked to complain that he and Walt Disney were the only two living people with parks named after them. He was reportedly embarrassed by the naming honor, but played there almost daily from the time the courts were built until his death, often with regular playing companions Larry Shippey, Bobby Dodd, Tom Bird, and Hank Crawford, into the 1980's. If he wasn't on the courts, he would be in the clubhouse playing checkers.

Bitsy had met Shippey after the war at the Piedmont Driving Club, where they both played. They compiled an incredible record of national titles together. Grant was several years older, and told Shippey he would wait for him to win the 45's. He did; and they did. They won four straight 45's nationals in 1960, 1961, 1962, and 1963; rested a few years and came back again to win two more, in 1965 and 1966, when Bitsy was then 55.

He continued to compete as a senior, winning 19 U.S. singles titles on the four surfaces: Grass Court 45's (1956 and 1957), 55's (1965, 1966, 1967 and 1968); Indoor 55's (1966); Clay Court 45's (1959, 1960, 1961 and 1963), 55's (1965, 1966, 1967, 1968 and 1969), 65's (1976 and 1977); and the Hard Court 65's (1976).

He regards his greatest win to be the quarters of the 1933 U.S. National Championships (later to be called the U S Open after 1968, when professionals were allowed to play it) when he beat Ellsworth Vines[1], at that time the No. 1 player in the world.

"I beat him in straight sets, 6-3, 6-3, 6-3. And the funny thing was, he had just beaten me in straight sets in Newport, 6-0, 6-3"

Shortly after master promoter Bobby Riggs hyped up his dog-and-pony circus maximus match up with Margaret Court (but before the one with Billie Jean King), the Racket Club of the South in Atlanta jumped on the band wagon and came up with pitting a girl in her teens against a legend in his 60's. Speculation about the outcome was rife and rampant, mostly that WTA playing pro Betsy Butler didn't stand a chance, and that the old master would prevail. Money went on the line, including a $500 purse, maybe more at show time, said director Fred Clouser. Bitsy's long time playing companion Tom Bird predicted that *"...Bitsy will kill her..."* It didn't work that way, and hard hitting serve-and-volleying Betsy prevailed with more power than the aging warrior could handle. Bitsy lamented later that he should never have agreed to the match. But it was too late.

He was inducted into the International Tennis Federation Hall of Fame in 1972, the Southern Tennis Hall of Fame in 1977, along with Hamilton Richardson; they were the first two players so honored; and later into the Collegiate Tennis Hall of Fame, the National Tennis Hall of Fame, and the Georgia Athletic Hall of Fame.

Still defying age, he entered the main draw of the 1982 Atlanta City Championship. He had just turned 71. A first round loss to the number 2 seed didn't phase him, but probably gave his opponent considerable anxiety.

---

[1] *Vines reportedly became bored with tennis in his late twenties, fell in love with golf, and won two major golf events in 1955, the Massachusetts and Utah Opens, playing as a professional.*

"My Dad was a creature of habit..."

"My mother and father divorced when I was two. Mother moved back in with her family, and it was decided that it would be better for my brother and I to live with Dad, because he was going to move in with his mother (my grandmother), and my Aunt Hattie.

"My grandmother's house was on Peachtree, right across from Christ The King church. It was me, my dad, my aunt, my brother, and my grandmother (who was also called Hattie).

"We had servants. Our maid was 'Ethyl', and our chauffeur when I was young was 'Albert.' Later we had another chauffeur, 'Cleveland.'

"He drove us to school in a big black Packard. My brother insisted on being dropped off 2 or 3 blocks from school to keep his friends from teasing him. I went off to boarding school for my 10th, 11th, and 12th grades.

"We always had money; my grandfather was very smart and made a lot of money and I think he sold his company to Adams Cates later on.

"My aunt and grandmother were always after my father about his social style. He hated cocktail parties and was very shy. He would far rather be out playing baseball with kids from across the tracks than going to some party. He was also very dependent and needed taking care of.

"My grandfather was a very good tennis player, and taught my father, but thought him too small to ever be able to play good, so it was up to

"My grandfather had a court in the backyard, and my grandmother lots of times had her friends over to play, and when they left she would hit with Dad.

"Later when he was 10 or 11 he started beating his older brother, my uncle Berry, so they started paying attention. His mother started having him "fill in", when he was around 8 or 9 when they needed a fourth, and of course he was better than all of them put together, so it became apparent then that he was going to be really good."

"Dad always had a convertible. He played his tennis at the Piedmont Driving Club where we were members, and sometimes on the Piedmont Park courts. He also liked squash, and played at the Driving Club, and he was a really good ping pong player. He loved all sports.

"My dad never re-married, but he had a long time girl friend, 'Eleanor', and they would go out to dinner twice a week, every Tuesday and Friday night, almost always to Mammy's Shanty, one of my dad's favorites. He was a creature of habit.

"He smoked cigarettes all his life, but it never seemed to affect his stamina.

"He told me that when he finished high school, my grandfather and grandmother first sent him to some military school for college, I'm not sure where it was.

He always told my brother and me that he spent a few days there and hated it, and caught the bus to U of NC. "

COURTESY MARY GRANT MACDONALD

Bitsy Grant in UNC blazer.

"His little dog "Snowball" was kind of an accident. Snowball was my dog. My dad loved dogs, but he never wanted dogs in the house, but for some reason he bonded with Snowball and took him everywhere. Once he took him to the grocery store, in the summertime, and to keep Snowball cool, he left him in the car with the air going and of course with the keys in the car. When he came out, the car was gone. He was very upset, and called us from the store. He didn't care about the car, just Snowball. They later found the car, stripped, tires gone, everything in the car taken, but Snowball was still right there on the front seat."

Mary Grant Macdonald
Atlanta, 2010

Bitsy, right,
with Don Budge, ca 1935

Bitsy, age 3

L-R Bitsy, with Tony Trabert
at the 1955 National Clay Court
Tournament at Bitsy Grant Tennis Center

Interviewed in 1972 at an "old player-young player" event in Florida, he was questioned about today's players and what they earn:

"I have no regrets - I made about $100,000 in 1939. That would be nothing today, but it was big money back then. I paid about $2000 in taxes, and had a lot left over. My expenses were paid, I stayed in the best hotels, ate at the best restaurants, and traveled all over the world. It was a good life, a fabulous ten years. I never thought about the money."

How would you do against today's players?

" Not so good. First, they're bigger. Look at what's happened in basketball and football. I think the day will come when we see players the size of Wilt Chamberlain in the game, and he will be just average. They may have to do something to change the game, because with players like that, the serve becomes dominant. He would be hitting down so hard, you couldn't see it coming. The game we played was quite different."

A few years later, in October 1977 after winning the National 65's Clay in California, he reminisced again about age and the changes in the game:

"If I can get four balls back nowadays, I'm doing good. If I played the Bitsy Grant of 1930 today, I would loose love and love. I've won 43 national titles, in every age group except the 35's. They didn't have a 35's when I would have been eligible."

ATLANTA JOURNAL-CONSTITUTION: 1/1/1983. USED BY PERMISSION. COPYRIGHT. SPECIAL COLLECTIONS AND ARCHIVES, GEORGIA STATE UNIVERSITY LIBRARY.

Above, Bitsy relaxing at on the porch in 1983, shirtless, watching the action on court one, the center named for him, perhaps having just come from work. The city of Atlanta enforces strictly their rule of "no shirt, no play," but Bitsy enjoyed a lifelong exemption.

"His shyness gave the impression he was being a little haughty," says Ernie Garrison, longtime Bitsy Grant Tennis Center player. *"He was just very quiet, very reserved."*

COURTESY DAN MAGILL

Above, Bitsy Grant at the 1971 NCAA Div I Singles final. Athens Ga. University of Georgia Coach Dan Magill prevailed on Bitsy to help out, here shown chairing a match between Trinity teammates Brian Gottfried and Dick Stockton.

COURTESY MARY GRANT MACDONALD

His Eskimo Spitz "Snowball" was his constant companion, the only dog allowed at Bitsy Grant Tennis Center.

A New York Times sports writer once observed that Grant, baseball's Ty Cobb and golfer Bobby Jones were the three greatest athletes ever to come out of a single state.

He and his wife Mary Cleveland had two children, Mary and Bryan III.

LARRY SHIPPEY
1916-2003

Enigma, Ga., (population 862) would not normally be regarded as the ideal birthplace for an athlete destined for national prominence. His family moved to Waycross when he was four, where he saw baseball and tennis for the first time. A natural athlete, he played baseball in high school, and as an outfielder he was mediocre but, as one observer put it, "*at bat he was something else.*"

With an eye for hitting and controlling a ball, tennis was a natural transition. "*...at first I got my brains beat out, but I kept working at it—the serve, the forehand, the backhand—and eventually it all fell into place.*" At age 18, he won the Waycross City Championship, then played two years at Georgia Southern in Statesboro, but became ineligible when he transferred to the University of Georgia. He continued to play in Athens at the city courts while pursuing his journalism degree.

Shippey on the court at
Bitsy Grant Tennis Center, 2001

After graduation, he joined his father in the automobile business, selling Hudsons. In 1940, when that business faded with the demise of the Hudson, his father opened an auto repair business and young Shippey joined the Navy.

He was assigned to Jacksonville Naval Air Station, and continued to play tennis, becoming the No. 1 player on the base. The Navy found him to be not just a very good pilot, but good enough to teach others. He became a flight instructor, and eventually found his way to the NAS at Chamblee, Georgia.

When the Piedmont Driving Club offered a special rate membership to military personnel he joined, and continued to hone his skills there, and eventually met and married Anne Owens, daughter of Frank Owens, a perennial Driving Club champion, and Anne and Larry became unbeatable when playing together.

He became acquainted with Bitsy Grant at the Driving Club, and he credits Grant with much of his success. They would later win many tournaments together. Later he would also win many with Russell Bobbitt, Tom Bird, Crawford Henry, and Bobby Dodd, including six USTA national titles and more city championships than he can remember.

Frank Owens

COURTESY BITSY GRANT TENNIS ASSOCIATION

One of Larry's most memorable matches was when he and Georgia Tech Coach Bobby Dodd defeated a nationally ranked doubles team, Whitney Reid and Gene Scott, in the Atlanta Invitational. They had devised a scheme, feigning ineptitude and missing shot after shot in the warm-up before the match. Its unlikely the ruse had anything at all to do with their victory, but it was hilarious, and the spectators went wild.

At Bitsy Grant Tennis Center Larry was known as the "savvy man" by the many boys he "coached for free" and whose advice helped several of them become champions, among them Crawford Henry, who went on to win the Southern men's singles and the NCAA doubles twice at Tulane and is a member of the Collegiate Hall of Fame; Allen Morris, Presbyterian College's finest player and a Wimbledon quarter-finalist in 1956; Bob Nichols, Georgia Tech All-American in 1959; and Richard Howell, Princeton star, and member of the Georgia Tennis Hall of Fame.

"Frank (Hop) Owens, had been a tennis star at Georgia Tech, and I was afraid Larry's son Bill would want to go there. Bill graduated from the Lovett School in Atlanta, where he was the state junior champion, and thankfully he decided on Georgia, he told me, because he had enjoyed playing on the UGA courts in the Crackerland tournament .

"He was the first recipient of a Georgia tennis scholarship and he won the SEC No. 1 freshman singles in 1966 and later teamed with Danny Birchmore to make Georgia a tennis power. 'Hop' Owens, was often in our stands cheering for his grandson, sitting next to Larry.

"After graduation, Bill became one of the best court builders around, and resurfaces our courts every year (to keep them 'Shippeyshape).'

Dan Magill 2010

COURTESY SOUTHERN TENNIS ASSOCIATION

Larry with son Bill

COURTESY COLLEGIATE TENNIS HALL OF FAME

"Red was an engineer who used a scientific approach to tennis. I remember seeing him at "Bitsy" years ago, during a tournament, on the porch overlooking court one where a match was being played, one foot hiked up on the rail at the top. He was educating me on stringing and weighting using using lead tape. He was holding the racket, facing upwards, his right hand reverently stroking gently here and there to illustrate his points. He explained why he used one tension for the mains, and another for the cross strings, and why the lead tape had to be put just so around the edges, and what it did. He wasn't alone; a lot of players put tape on their rackets, particularly the "court one" crowd at "Bitsy."

"I tried it, and all it did was make my racket heavy. I had no clue what I was looking for. But he was ahead of his time. Several manufacturers now even make lead weights specifically designed to be inserted into various cavities in the racket, and many rackets now are classified as "head heavy" or "head light.".

"He did his own stringing, with a broomstick and an awl, rolling the broomstick to get it tight and plucking the string to hear the sound it made. Tennis voodoo? Who knows. But it gave him confidence
Author

ARTHUR ENLOE
1905-1977

Known as "Red", he was the first winner of the National 65's Senior Clay, ever. The division had just been created by the USTA in 1968, and Red swept the singles and doubles. He followed that by winning the doubles in the event for the next three years straight. The singles winners that followed him were Bitsy Grant, Gardner Mulloy, and Bobby Riggs.

He played tennis when his family moved to Atlanta in 1915, but never made his mark in the sport until after retiring. He graduated from Atlanta's Tech High, and attended Georgia Tech until WWII carried him to the South Pacific, building military bases and airstrips, where he found time to play tennis for an Army inter-service team.

After the war he played at the Atlanta Tennis Club on Argonne Ave. until it closed after sale of the land. "Bitsy" had just been built and he played often there, living in Decatur and working for the DeKalb County Water Department as its Chief Engineer.

He was instrumental in lobbying for the construction of DeKalb Tennis Center. He was familiar with the site of the courts, which had long been the water source for DeKalb's Druid Hills area when the Olmstead Parks were created.

When he retired in 1970, he became serious about tennis, and trained in earnest, often 4 or more hours a day. It paid off. He won the National 70's hard court singles in 1972 and 1973 and the National 70's grass singles in 1972 and the doubles in 1975, his ninth and final national title. He died of a heart attack in the middle of a finals match in Ft. Myers, Florida, in 1977. He is recognized in the International Tennis Hall of Fame in Newport, RI, and is a member of the Georgia and Southern Tennis Halls of Fame.

DR. NAT THORNTON

The oldest picture at Bitsy Grant Tennis Center in Atlanta has been there since the center was built in 1952. Nat Thornton was a player of national prominence in the early twentieth century. In 1908, he held a national singles (USLTA) ranking of 34.

In 1906 and 1907, Dr. Thornton and B.M. Grant (Bitsy Grant's father) won the Southern Doubles, and in 1907 were runners-up in the men's open doubles at the U.S. National Championships. In 1912, in the "Preliminary National Doubles Ties" in Lake Forest IL, Thornton and his partner that year, Carleton Y. Smith of Atlanta, representing the South, were defeated in the finals.

He won the Southern Championship Singles in 1907, 1908, and again in 1913, in New Orleans, Louisiana, defeating that year fellow Georgian Carlton Smith.

In August 1915, Thornton and B. M. Grant teamed up to play in the "Elimination Doubles", representing the South, one of five teams competing for the privilege of playing the incumbent champions in the National Championships at the West Side Tennis Club in Forest Hills, N.Y. in September. They won the Southern Doubles that year, and again in 1918.

In August 1920, he and B.M. Grant won a first round match in the "Open Championships of Georgia" at the Atlanta Athletic Club against R. W. Courts and Harry Hallman.

Nat Thornton graduated from Georgia Tech, Class of 1910.

Nat Thornton and trophies

HANK CRAWFORD
1910-1995

Hank Crawford was left an orphan at age 9. He went to live with an older sister in College Park, Ga., and in investigating, as a curious young boy, the Cox College athletic supply room, he found tennis equipment stored there. He began playing.

As a student at Russell High, he was unbeaten until running into another Atlanta boy, Bryan Grant, with whom he would win, many years later, his first national title, the USLTA National Mens' 55's Indoor. While attending Georgia Tech, he lettered in basketball and tennis and won the Southeastern Conference singles title in 1934. After graduation from Tech, he went to Woodrow Wilson law school and later became City Attorney for College Park.

WWII interrupted his tennis, and he did not return until 1957, after a layoff of 15 years. His best tennis years were ahead of him. He would win 12 U.S. national titles, with partners Grant, Len Prosser, and Tom Bird, and later would play for the U.S. Britannia Cup team on the European Senior circuit with Gardner Mulloy.

He was inducted into the Southern Tennis and Georgia Athletic Halls of Fame. Before Bitsy Grant Tennis Center was built, he played at the Atlanta Tennis Club, and then switched to "Bitsy," where he played regularly until the day before his death. Court One at the center is named for him. He was the first president of the Atlanta Lawn Tennis Association.

He and partner Tom Bird, playing in the National Hardcourt 60's doubles in Santa Barbara CA, stunned Bobby Riggs and partner Allen Doyle with unexpected defeat (the third for Bird/Crawford over Riggs). At one while time ranked nationally No. 1 in the 60's doubles, they were also ranked No. 2 in the 55's, and No. 3 in the 50's.

"We played some good teams out there. Nobody thought a team from the East could win by lobbing. We were pretty good at it. We would lob until they got tired."

Together they won 12 National titles.

COURTESY BITSY GRANT TENNIS ASSOCIATION

TOM BIRD

Tom came to Atlanta from Kentucky in the 1930's with his wife. He had been a basketball player in high school, and became interested in tennis, playing on the weekends at the Northside Tennis Club on Argonne Ave., until Bitsy Grant Tennis Center opened. There he met and forged a lifelong tennis partnership with Hank Crawford. His forte' was enough speed to run around his backhand and hit a hard flat forehand, nicknamed "Big Bertha" by his companions.

After retirement from the Dekalb County Water System, he concentrated on tennis, and teamed up occasionally with either Bobby Dodd, Bitsy Grant, or Larry Shippey. A calculator is needed to tote up his titles; counting the regional and nine national ones, he has more than 50. He is the first Georgian (before Bitsy Grant even) to win a "grand slam," national titles on all four surfaces in a single year.

1973 brought a couple of hiccups to nationally known player Bobby Riggs. First, playing with partner Al Doyle, he was beaten (for the second time) by Bird and partner Hank Crawford in the USTA 55's indoor nationals finals, after having stated that he could bury both Bird and Crawford in singles, "love and love." His excuse was, "*...the sun was in our eyes...*" Chalk one up for a couple of expert lobbers

A few months later, Riggs went down before Billie Jean King after considerable public hype. His first spanking by Bird/Crawford had come two years earlier, in 1971, in the semis of the National Clay 50's in Knoxville, when his partner was Chauncey Steele (34 national titles). Tom considered this his best career win.

In one year, 1973, he was ranked nationally No. 3 or better in three age divisions, the 50's, 55's, and 60's. In 1971, he and partner Bobby Dodd were ranked No. 3 in the Georgia 35's - - when Bird was 58, and Dodd 61, giving up almost 30 years against most opponents going in. He earned a No. 1 Southern singles ranking in every age division from the 55's through the 75's. He was a finalist in the 1966 USTA National Clay 45's, at age 53.

MALON COURTS

Malon Courts was one of three founders of the Atlanta Lawn Tennis Association, in 1934. The purpose of the organization at that time was to promote tennis tournaments and junior tennis development in the Atlanta area. "ALTA," as it became known much later, started league play in 1971 with less than 1,000 members, and grew to almost 10,000 in 1975, 35,000 in 1982, over 51,000 in 1988 and 71,000 in 1992. Today it's approaching 100,000 members. It evolved from a small group of volunteers to a large non-profit corporation recognized by tennis players around the world.

COURTESY SOUTHERN TENNIS ASSOCIATION

Courts was an accomplished athlete, lettering in basketball and tennis at the University of Georgia, and winning the Southern Conference singles title in 1927. In the 1937 Atlanta Invitational, he lost a close second round match to Bobby Riggs, 7-5, 6-4. That same year, he reached the quarters of the Georgia State Championships. He remained active in the game, and in 1954, he won the Southern Senior singles. He teamed with Bryan Grant to win the National Clay Courts Senior Men's doubles in 1955.

Off court, he enjoyed extraordinary business success, and was a partner in the investment banking firm of Courts and Company. He played tennis regularly at the Piedmont Driving Club. His vision for the game, however, was to expand it beyond private clubs, and he was the driving force in the construction of Bitsy Grant Tennis Center. The Mayor of Atlanta at that time was William B. Hartsfield, whom Courts approached with a bold demand for 15 acres next to Bobby Jones Golf Course on Northside Drive, and $250,000 to build a tennis complex. The first response was something like, *"...I have more important business, please leave..."*

COURTESY GEORGIA TENNIS HALL OF FAME

The mayor underestimated Courts' persistence, and two years later, the center became a reality, making tennis in Atlanta a sport for all economic levels. He passed away in 1957, dying of a heart attack on the court at the Piedmont Driving Club.

Playing at Northside Tennis
Club, Atlanta ca 1920

> *"In my second season as Georgia's coach, I invited Malon to sit with me during a match against Georgia Tech in Atlanta, and give me some doubles pointers. His son Richard was playing for us at the time. He knew far more than I did about doubles, and told me we had to concentrate on offense, taking the net at every opportunity. It changed my coaching strategy considerably from that day forward. "*
>
> *Dan Magill, 2009*

LOUISE FOWLER
1907-1979

Mary Louise Fowler was the first woman to be inducted into the Georgia Tennis Hall of Fame. She began playing at age 8, but didn't take it seriously until she entered Agnes Scott College in Decatur, GA. She went on to earn a masters degree at the University of Georgia, and returned to teach biology at Oxford College in Covington, her home town. She consistently earned a high Southern ranking, the highest being No. 1 in doubles from 1944 to 1959, with four different partners.

She and Natalie Cohen won the Georgia State Open Doubles six straight times, from 1947 to 1952. She played regularly with tennis student and hometown friend Evelyn Cowan, together winning the Crackerland doubles so many times that Dan Magill called them *"the best doubles team to ever play in the tournament."* She played in virtually all the states in the Southern region. In 1958 she swept all the NC events, winning the singles, doubles, and mixed doubles in Ashville. She is a member of both the Georgia Tennis and the Georgia Sports Halls of Fame.

Fowler, left, winner of 1954 Crackerland Open Doubles, with (L to R) Covington friend and tennis pupil Evelyn Cowan; and runners-up Billie Wickliffe and June Bryson.

VINCE CONNERAT
1910-2005

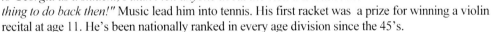
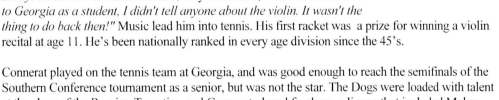

In September 2000, Connerat (AB '31, University of Georgia.) continued his dominance of the most senior division of the USTA by winning the 90-and-over singles in the U.S. National Grass Courts at the famed Longwood Cricket Club outside Boston.

When the Charlotte, NC, resident wasn't stroking a tennis ball, he was playing first violin in the Queen's College Community Orchestra. *"I've always loved both tennis and music,"* says Connerat, *"But when I came to Georgia as a student, I didn't tell anyone about the violin. It wasn't the thing to do back then!"* Music lead him into tennis. His first racket was a prize for winning a violin recital at age 11. He's been nationally ranked in every age division since the 45's.

Connerat played on the tennis team at Georgia, and was good enough to reach the semifinals of the Southern Conference tournament as a senior, but was not the star. The Dogs were loaded with talent at the close of the Roaring Twenties, and Connerat played far down a lineup that included Malon Courts (AB '29), John Beaver (AB '33), and Jack Boykin (MA '32). As it turned out, his best days as a tennis player were ahead of him. *"For the first 25 years after I graduated, I couldn't play much tennis,"* says Connerat, who was an economist for HUD, the Bureau of Labor Statistics, and the U.S. Department of Commerce.

" I've never been sick a day in my life. I feel now (at 85) the same as I did at 50"

DON FLOYD
1915-2001

Hanging on the "Wall of Champions" at Bitsy over the stairs going down to the locker rooms is a fading photo (right), with no information beyond the name. Its unlikely many who see it would recognize the player.

And none would guess that at one point in his career, he would have a win over the No. 1 player in the world. That happened in the 1943, at the N.C. State Open, when he beat Wilmer Allison,[1] who just a few years before had brought down the great Bitsy Grant at the height of his career in straight sets in 1936 in the Atlanta Invitational at the Biltmore Tennis Club. Allison had the year before won the 1935 U.S. Championship singles (later to become, the U.S. Open), defeating Fred Perry. Floyd was a linesman for the Allison/Grant match. He was 21 and the part-time manager of the Club, working regularly for the Railway Express Company. He stayed with them for 33 years. His passion for tennis began at age 17 in Atlanta, where his family moved, from Charlotte, NC, when he was 5

In 1942, an Atlanta paper reported on a tennis exhibition to be played at the Northside Tennis Club, the feature event being a "grudge match" between brothers-in-law Don Floyd and Nat Collins. It stated that Floyd had eliminated Collins in a recent tournament, that Collins was "seeking revenge," and that the two players had arranged a side bet on the outcome, the looser being required to push Atlanta tennis enthusiast Mollie Williamson, all 315 pounds of him, in a wheelbarrow, from the Northside Tennis Club on North Ave. to Ponce de Leon Ave., several blocks away. There is no record of the winner. Statistically Floyd would have been favored. The distance would be half a mile, uphill. A heavy bet.

L-R, Cortez Suttles, Hank Crawford, Marine Corp Lt. Alice MacDonald, Marjorie Waite, and Floyd in the Southern Championships, 1935, at the Northside Tennis Club in Atlanta

Floyd, front row left, with Georgia Evening School[2] teammates, 1943

[1] *Donna Floyd Fales stated in 2010 that her father always regarded this as the most significant win of his career.*
[2] *Now known as Georgia State University.*

In 1937, a prominent tennis coach of the day, Eleanor Tennant, came to Atlanta to conduct a clinic. A highly regarded California teaching pro, she had been credited with boosting Alice Marble's (U.S. Women's Champion 4 years, Wimbledon Womens' Open once) game to another level with a grip change from "western" to "eastern." Floyd, then 22, was in the audience, and asked a question regarding his grip, to which Tennant replied *"I'd advise you to change, but I'm afraid you're past tournament age..."* Tennant may have known something about grips, but not much about judging talent.

He later attended Georgia Evening School, which allowed pursuing a college degree while continuing to work. He played on the tennis team there from 1939-1944, as captain, manager and No. 1 player, and the team was undefeated those years. He continued to play tournaments, and in 1942 he won the Georgia State Singles, defeating Jack Teagle in the finals.

His most memorable win, however, would be the 1943 match against Wilmer Allison in the NC State Open. In 1947, he won the Cotton States Singles, and in 1948, 1949, and 1951 the Pensacola Invitational Singles, whose prior winners include Bobby Riggs; in 1950 the Mobile Invitational and the Northeast Georgia Singles Championships; and in 1955, at age 40, the Atlanta City Championship Singles and the Virginia State Men's Open Singles, defeating many younger players, some half his age. That same year, daughter Donna won the Virginia State Women's open division at age 15. The Floyd family had moved to Arlington Virginia in 1953. He was ranked nationally as high as number 10.

In the 1965 U S Championships in Forest Hills at the West Side Tennis Club, daughter Donna was playing in the Womens' Open division, Don playing in the 45's. A newspaper reported that *"...Mrs. Donald Floyd had a strenuous few hours one day when her husband and daughter played on adjoining courts...separated by a pathway for spectators. Husband Don was playing a close three set match against Robert Lemke Jr. of Philadelphia on one court, while across the aisle daughter Donna was meeting Peachy Kellmeyer of Charleston, WV. Mrs. Floyd would watch Don for a game or two, then cross the aisle to follow her daughter's match..."*

Overall, he played over 1000 tournaments, winning 200 titles, mostly singles. Later he became a certified USPTA professional. He was inducted into Washington Capitol Tennis Hall of Fame in 1981.

Always active in promoting tennis, Floyd served on the boards of numerous organizations, including the Atlanta Lawn Tennis Association, the Georgia State Tennis Association, the Southern Tennis Association, the Virginia State Tennis Association, the Arlington Virginia Tennis Association, the Washington, DC Tennis Association, and the Middle Atlantic Tennis Association. He passed away in 2001 in Fort Lauderdale, FL, where he had lived for 18 years.

RUSSELL BOBBIT
1918-2005

Bobbitt grew up in Atlanta not far from the tennis courts at Georgia Tech. As a boy, he hung out there, occasionally being asked to fill in. He was a Georgia State Junior Champion and played on the Georgia Tech Team (class of 1940). He won the Southeastern Conference Doubles Championship (with partner Bill Moore) in 1938, helping his school win the team competition.

He reached the semis of the U.S. Championships in 1940, and played numerous events with Bitsy Grant as his partner. He was inducted into the Georgia Tech Athletics Hall of Fame in 1958, and the Southern Tennis Hall of Fame in 1993.

Above, after a 1945 exhibition match at the All England Club, being presented medals by the Duchess of Kent, flanked by His Worship the Mayor of Wimbledon. Bobbitt is in the far right of the picture. War with Germany had halted the Wimbledon Championships for six years, and on this occasion, Bobbitt was a member of the U.S. armed forces team that played a team representing Great Britain. It was the first match played at Wimbledon since 1939.

> *"Maj. Gen. Albert Jones was Georgia's tennis coach, and he had asked me (in 1952, I was then the school's sports information director) to help promote the dedication ceremonies of Georgia's new varsity courts just south of Sanford Stadium. So I invited the state's four best players (all Atlantians) - Bryan (Bitsy) Grant, Frank Willett, Jack Teagle and Russell Bobbitt - to participate. Bobbitt and Willett, both former SEC champions at Georgia Tech, defeated Grant and Teagle 6-4, 6-1."*
>
> *Dan Magill*

NAT COLLINS

Nat is remembered by many as the proprietor of "The Tennis Shop," in Atlanta's Buckhead section on Pharr Road. It was a small store but packed with equipment, and did not sell anything not related to tennis.

Donald Floyd (Georgia Tennis Hall of Fame) and Nat Collins married sisters, Billye and Evelyn. Don chose a "regular job," with Railway Express, playing tennis in his off time, but Nat never got away from it, playing, teaching, operating his shop, running tennis facilities, and later stringing at tournaments for pros.

A natural athlete, he was awarded a football scholarship to Marist College[1]. He played every sport except tennis growing up, and said later he thought it was a *sissy sport*," but began spending time at Atlanta's Northside Tennis Club, which was near his home, and playing. He later ran Northside, earning $3.50/hour for lessons, about what a bank teller would then make. He gave up the job for a year in order to play on the Southern Lawn Tennis Association's Junior Davis Cup team, so strict were the rules then for amateur status. Not even writing articles for a magazine or newspaper or working in a sporting goods store was allowed.

He later opened his shop and made it his livelihood. He gave lessons to many Atlantian's, and in between, became good enough to be consistently ranked in Georgia in his age group.

During the era of Lamar Hunt's World Championship Tennis, he strung rackets for the players, traveling from tournament to tournament. Often under contract with Spalding, Wilson, Dunlop, and others, his strings were winning matches for John MacEnroe, Guillermo Villas, Vitas Geralaitis, and others at the pinnacle of the sport at the time. He had a sizeable staff, at one point employing 25 stringers, mostly Georgia Tech students. Players who patronized his shop in Buckhead will recall it was like going back in time; the walls were covered with photographs and memorabilia of all kinds, especially old rackets. One of them was a 1930's model Mercer-Beasley used by Bitsy Grant when he earned a No. 3 world ranking in 1938. The shop was one of just a few that continued to stock "gut" for stringing after nylon strings became popular.

Collins' daughter Mary became a skillful player, earning a No. 1 ranking in the Georgia Girls' 18's. In 1987 and 1988, she traveled with the mens' pro tour, working as a travel agent, booking all air and hotel accommodations for the players. And in some cases for their girl friends, sometimes, incredibly, different ones from week to week. The job required discretion and sealed lips.

Mary Collins
Photo by the author

[1] *Marist was a high school, then located in downtown Atlanta, on Ivy St.; it's now known as the "Marist School," co-ed, and located on Ashford Dunwoody Road*

OSCAR T. MULLIS
1931-2009

Known as "Sonny" all his life, he grew up in Atlanta and played tennis early on, becoming one of the most outstanding amateurs in the state. In high school he won numerous state GIAA championships, both doubles and singles, and throughout his life was always highly ranked in his age group. He was a regular player at Bitsy Grant Tennis Center, and was well known there. A natural classic shotmaker, his extraordinary placement and accuracy brought many heavy hitters down to defeat.

He never won his age group in Kalamazoo, at the USTA National Juniors, but the records show many wins there. In an era when tennis scholarships were rare, he had two offers, one to Young Harris, in the foothills of the Georgia mountains, which he took, and one to Presbyterian College, which he declined. Had he been inclined to spend the money later in life, to travel and play in national events, he would unquestionably have won many titles. On May 10, 1959, tennis legend Fred Perry came to town, and an exhibition match was staged at Bitsy Grant Tennis Center, featuring Perry and Bitsy Grant vs Sonny and Jack Rogers, then the pro at the center. Jack and Sonny eked out a win, 6-4, 3-6, 7-5. Not many players can claim a victory over Grant, nor Perry.

MULLIS FAMILY COLLECTION, COURTESY MARTHA KELLEY

> *"I grew up watching his smooth stroking, totally natural and effortless. I doubt he ever had a lesson. He was one of those rare individuals that can figure it out on their own and make it work.*
>
> *"Allen Morris told me, recalling in 2009 Sonny's style, when they were in high school, '...I could never beat him with the way I played then (a power game); he would just stand back there and place it wherever he wanted, without any effort, smooth but solid stroking, keep me moving around, and eventually I would make an error...'*
>
> *"Sonny dominated a lot of hard hitters that way. His accuracy was uncanny. His movement on the court seemed effortless, never straining, never off balance. I remember one of the trips to Athens, Ga., venue of the GIAA in the '40's, he rode in my car with several of us. He won it, as he did most years. That trip stands out in my memory because I got a speeding ticket on the way home, going through Decatur."*
>
> *Author*

GEORGE RAMEY PENDLEY

Pendley grew up in At-
lanta, on Penn Avenue,
close to the intersection
of Ponce de Leon and
Peachtree St., next door
to legendary Georgia
Tech football coach
Bobby Dodd.

He learned to play on the
clay courts at Piedmont
Park, and became good enough to play on the
Atlanta Boys High team. He enrolled at the
University of Georgia in 1942. Tennis had
been suspended because of the war, so he
played baseball, and became a starting pitcher.
He joined the Navy after 2 years at Georgia,
serving in the Pacific, and went back to Georgia at war's end, where he played on the Georgia tennis team for 3 years.

His best tennis was long after college, as a
senior player, starting with a win at the Crackerland at age 35. He went on to win six more
Crackerlands, twelve Georgia State tournaments, six City of Atlanta titles, five Southern
titles, and many other tournaments in Georgia
and surrounding states. His biggest win was
the USTA National Clay 55's doubles, in
1980, with partner Gus Palafox.

Before and after that he won many Georgia
and Southern district tournaments with many
different partners.

He battled joint problems and bone cancer for
years but continued to play through his infir-
mities. He had many interests; music, cooking,
fine wines, journalism (BA, UGA, journalism) and was a passionate fisherman.

*"Pendley is a medical miracle ...sometimes
playing with excruciating pain from bone cancer...as I write these words, I wonder if he will
be alive to read them..."*
                    Gene Asher, "Legends..."

GEORGE AMAYA
1950-2006

Amaya was born in Wey-
mouth, Mass., and lived in
New England until his fa-
ther, Jaime, moved his family to his native Colombia when
George was five.

He would become the No. 2 junior player in the country with little formal training, just a love of tennis that
he shared with his father and six siblings. *"We were
students of the game,"* Amaya said." *Any time there
was exhibition, like when Rod Laver, Fred Stolle, or
other great players came to Colombia, us kids would
just kill to go and watch them and take notes and try
to emulate how they played."* One of Amaya's fondest
memories as a teenager was working as a volunteer
line judge in the singles final of an event in Colombia.
The finalists were Tony Roche and John Newcombe.

Amaya followed brothers Jim and Juan to Presbyterian College in Clinton, S.C., and won the NAIA
singles and doubles titles in 1971.

He spent two years in the military and two in coaching before attempting the pro circuit at age 25. In his
first pro event, he made the semifinals of singles and
the finals of doubles in New Zealand. *"For the doubles prize money, I got an envelope with a note that
said, 'Prize money $5, Entry fee $4.50;' ...inside there
was a 50-cent coin; that's when I realized the circuit
was going to be tough."*

Amaya got as high as No. 170 in the world, and
played the U.S. Open three times. After retiring, he
remained one of Atlanta's elite players, and for many
years was director of tennis at Atlanta's Cherokee
Town and Country Club. He was a four-time singles
champion and six-time doubles winner of the Atlanta
Senior Invitational, which attracts more senior national champions than any other tournament in the
U.S. He passed away at age 55, from cancer, at his
Atlanta residence.

*"I'd like for people to remember me for my sense of
enjoyment for the game,"* Amaya said, *"but also that
when I did compete, I did it with a high level of
sportsmanship and respect for my opponent and for
tennis."*

                    George Amaya, 2005

NATALIE COHEN
1912-2007

Some who follow amateur tennis know Natalie's accomplishments on the court; many remember her more recently as a USTA umpire. She did it for over fifty years. She was the first woman to serve in the chair for a men's NCAA Championship; and the first southern woman to serve as a chair umpire at the U.S. Open. At the time the tournament was still held at the West Side Tennis Club in Forest Hills, N Y. Her recognition as an umpire include the Marlborough Award from World Tennis in 1962; umpire of the year by the Southern Tennis Association in 1976; the Jacobs Bowl award in 1977; the Georgia Tennis Association umpire of the year award in 1978; and the Georgia Tennis Association Service Award in 1980. She was inducted into the Southern Tennis Association, Georgia Tennis Association and Georgia Jewish Sports Halls of Fame, and received the Presidential Sports Award, presented by President Gerald Ford.

She was the first woman to umpire a professional match, that during the Jack Kramer tours in the 1950s. Once she made national headlines when she reprimanded professional player Ili Nastase, sending the volatile Romanian into a rage. The next day he thrilled the crowd by publicly apologizing, on bended knee, proffering a bouquet of roses, which she accepted.

She was ubiquitous in Atlanta tennis, somehow just being there at every significant event, a smile on her face, something to say to everyone. She was a friendly gregarious person.

COURTESY BETSY GRANT TENNIS ASSOCIATION

When she retired from playing tournaments in 1994, she had won thirteen Georgia State Women's Open Doubles Championships and the Atlanta City Open singles in 1949. In 1954, at age forty-two, she won the "grand slam" of local tennis by winning both the Atlanta City and Georgia State singles and doubles championships. Cohen was ranked at the time number two in doubles by the Southern Tennis Association.

She was a tireless tennis organizer and served as tournament director for countless events. She was the secretary/treasurer of the Atlanta Lawn Tennis Association for 25 years, and in 1967 was named Executive Director of the Southern Tennis Association, a post she held for 13 years.

Born on June 9, 1912, she was educated in the Atlanta public school system and attended Inman elementary, Bass Junior High, and Girls High (later to become Roosevelt High in 1947) from which she graduated in 1930. She then matriculated at University of California, Berkeley, graduating with a bachelor of arts degree in political science in 1934, with honors. She was such an ardent fan and booster that years later the university named a seat for her in the section of the football stadium where she cheered as a student.

See also p. 123

In 1986, she played a key role in a now historic Stanford-Cal football game. The Cal-Berkeley Bears were serious underdogs; 1-9 for the season, a head coach who had been fired three weeks earlier, a quarterback who hadn't started a game all season, and an offense that hadn't scored a touchdown in nearly a month. David Ortega, at the time a Cal linebacker (later the compliance director in the Cal athletic department) recalls that Cal coach Joe Kapp called on 74 year old Natalie Cohen, a well known alum and fan, to give a pre-game pep talk to the team.

It worked. "... *We ran out on the field together, as a team...*" Final: Cal 17, Stanford 11, the biggest upset victory in the Bears' history.

She was passionate about other sports as well. She once told Atlanta Braves' Bobby Cox that the Braves didn't bunt enough. She was a Hawks and Flames season ticket holder and attended nearly every Final Four basketball tournament for years. A true Atlanta tennis legend and a credit to the game.

"I'll never forget Natalie. I don't follow tennis but I'll always remember my accidental meeting with her. My mother was changing her will in her declining years, and we needed a witness, and somehow Natalie's office was close by. She did it willingly. After my mother's death I had to contact the witnesses for signing some papers. Our deal was, she would meet me at Lenox square at 11 am, I was to buy coffee. We did, and our meeting turned into a four hour lunch. She was a great conversationalist; about our families, her love of lobster and Forrest Hills, and of our summer place in Gloucester. I arranged to have 3 big ones, live, delivered to her at Christmas. I kept sending them until she passed away, even after she had lost her memory of our first contact. What a great lady."

Larry Jones, 2009

"She always seemed to be at the sign-in desk at every tournament I went to, handing out balls and court assignments. For years I never watched her play; while I wasn't looking she was quietly racking up an amazing record as a player. The thing I remember best, though, was that smile, always on top of the world.

"None of us thought of her as wealthy. She appeared to live frugally. We were all stunned to learn that she had left over two million dollars to the University of Georgia, with whom she had had a life long love affair, and a like amount to Cal-Berkeley."

Author

JACK WATERS

His tennis career began in 1934 as a 13-year-old in Miami, Florida. Captain of his high school team, he received a tennis scholarship to the University of Miami.[1]

His professional career began after 4 years in the Air Force during World War II and included matches against such prominent professional players as Jack Kramer and Bobby Riggs.

In 1950, he reached the quarter finals of both the singles and doubles at the U.S. National Clay Court Championships; his expense reimbursement as an amateur was $14.00. Those close to Jack believe that he would have enjoyed playing on the pro tour for several years, but he felt responsible for his mother and needed a steady income to help support her.

Waters was recruited in 1951 by Atlanta's Piedmont Driving Club member Lindsey Hopkins Jr.[2] as head pro for the club; that same year, Westminster, a new school in Atlanta, was formed, and Waters became the coach. He went far beyond just putting in nine to five. Among other things, he personally drove his young protégé's to tournaments he deemed essential for their development.

In 1952, five of the six top ranked players in the Boys 15's in the South were under his guidance. For the next ten years, the school dominated high school tennis in Georgia, culminating with winning the National Interscholastic title in 1956. In 1953, five of Jack's students reached the quarterfinals of the Southern Junior Tennis Tournament. Fifty-four of his students played on college tennis teams, thirty-four receiving tennis scholarships. Twenty were team captains and most were All Americans. Six have successfully competed as touring pros, and thirteen now teach others to play.

---

[1] UM was one of the earliest tennis powerhouses. They began granting scholarships in 1935, the first one to tennis legend Gardnar Mulloy, who organized and coached the team as a student, and promoted the construction of the school's tennis stadium. Mulloy was followed during the war years by Pancho Segura.

[2] Hopkins figured prominently in tennis in later years. His son Lindsey III was Captain of the University of Georgia tennis team in the 1950's; later, in 1980, being told by Coach Magill of the need for an indoor practice facility, he funded the Hopkins Indoor at the Dan Magill complex, with four courts and seating for 1200. It has often been used when inclement weather disrupts play during NCAA finals when played in Athens.

COURTESY SOUTHERN TENNIS

Such a prodigious output of talent was not the norm for a club pro at the time, and is more akin to the "tennis academies" of today. Had his player development system been the modern one with little or no schooling mixed in, perhaps most of them would have made the tour, but that would not have flown with Dr. Pressly at Westminster. Jack Waters was inducted into the Georgia Tennis Hall of Fame in 1985 and into the Dade County Florida Hall of Fame in 1988.

And he was generous. His Jack Waters Endowment Fund has granted over $65,000 to aspiring Georgia tennis players to pursue their dreams to the play the tour.

Upon the 93rd anniversary of the Piedmont Driving Club, the club's newsletter posted a tribute to his years there, reading, (in part):

"Though he would never admit it, the Piedmont Driving Club must have seemed a bit strange to Jack Waters when he surveyed...its facilities for the first time on that warm day in May of 1950. It was certainly different from Miami's La Gorce Country Club where he spent his early years as a tennis pro. Escorted by Athletic Chairman E. K. Van Winkle and Club Superintendent William Yohannan, what Jack observed would undoubtedly seem strange to us today... swimming commanded more attention in those days, and the old rectangular pool seemed to be the navel of all outdoor activity... a long screened porch flanked the entire pool side of the Ballroom where members would dine in an atmosphere of summer steam and chlorine fumes produced by a score or more electric fans... the pool empire was in the iron grip of Karo Whitfield,[1] our life guard at the time...

"Then, walking around a sawhorse barrier on the drive and past the impenetrable ten-foot high hedge which protected the swimming area from the rest of the world and through a maze of diagonally parked cars, Jack finally saw the five red clay courts for the first time... aside from a couple of ball boys on the courts, (among them future Georgia Tennis Hall of Fame member Branch Currington) ... there appeared to be no one else on the tennis staff...

"Could this be the future Olympus of Tennis he had envisioned after being recruited by Tennis Chairman Lindsey Hopkins, Jr.? ...One of the players Jack met that first day was the late Jolie Richardson, daughter of Mr. and Mrs. Hugh Richardson. It was irony indeed, that fourteen-year-old Jolie became Jack's first pupil at the "Gentlemen's Driving Club". Jolie, though already an accomplished player, went on to become PDC Ladies Champion two years in a row, and then captured the Georgia State Girls Championship four years in a row beginning in 1950, and won the PDC Mixed Doubles Championship with Frank Willet twice in a row. In 1953, she played in the Girls National Championship in Philadelphia and was invited to tryouts for the Junior Wightman Cup Team... Thus, Jack's first pupil contributed greatly to making his vision come true..."

---

[1] *Whitfield was officially the physical therapist and trainer at the club. He was active in weight lifting, and had his own gym on Forsyth St., near the Paramount Theatre.*

LINDSEY HOPKINS III
1936-2004
TWO FOR ONE FOR UGA

The first of the two was his exceptional talent. A superb junior player, he won the state collegiate singles and doubles twice, with partner Alfred Thompson Jr. The two also won the Eastern Intercollegiate freshman doubles. He captained the University of Georgia team in his senior year. One thing will never be forgotten; his remarkable volleying ability. It will be remembered because an annual award is given to the UGA player most proficient in volleying.

The second was a loving, devoted, and proud father, Lindsey Jr., who left his mark on Georgia tennis in the form of the Hopkins Indoor Courts, said by Coach Magill to have been the biggest factor in UGA becoming a national power in collegiate tennis—allowing the team to practice year round, rain or shine. At the time the facility was one of only three such collegiate layouts in the country.

It could easily have turned out differently because Lindsey Jr. started his college education at the University of Alabama, switching after one quarter to the University of Georgia, beginning, in his words, "*a still long continuing love affair...I had three of the most glorious years of my life here.*" Lindsey Hopkins Jr., aka "Big Lindsey", was a shrewd and extremely successful businessman. He parlayed his involvement in automobile sales (his father had moved to Atlanta from Greensboro, NC, to open a dealership) into banking and investments, becoming at one point one of the largest holders of Coca-Cola stock, allowing him financial running room for his pursuit of such diverse things as motor sports and tennis.

Lindsey Hopkins III

Lindsey Jr. often had two entries in the Indianapolis 500, finishing second three times. He was inducted into the Indianapolis 500 Hall of Fame posthumously in 2004. His fascination with tennis led to his chairing the Southern Junior Davis Cup Committee, and in giving a jump start to the tennis program at the Piedmont Driving Club by bringing Jack Waters from Miami to head it up, leading to a flood of talented junior players dominating amateur junior tournaments for a long time. The four court indoor facility at UGA was financed entirely by him in 1970, several years after his son had played for the team. At his death in 1986, Jesse Outlar's tribute in the Atlanta Constitution read "*He was one of the last of a vanishing breed of true sportsmen...*"

Lindsey Hopkins Jr.

"*Over 50 years ago, Lindsey Hopkins III walked into my life and never left. He came with his tennis coach, Jack Waters, to play in the Crackerland tournament, and won his age division, the first of many....When I became coach (at UGA)...we didn't have scholarships...but most of the best young players in the state were protégés of Jack Waters and sons of wealthy alumni...they didn't need scholarships...their allowances were larger than the entire (school's) budget for tennis.*"

Dan Magill, "*Oral History of the University of Georgia*"

See also p. 141

EDGAR A. NEELY III (NED)
1940-1999

In the mid 1950's, Earl Bortell, tennis coach since 1934 at Georgia Tech, along with Tech's iconic Dean George Griffin, recruited several prominent junior players for the team, including Neely. In 1960, Ned and teammate Bob Nichols made All-American; and with David Peake, Harry Thompson, Dave Pearsall and Paul Metz they captured the Georgia. Intercollegiate Championship and the SEC Championship.

Growing up, it was clear he would become a world class player. He was nationally ranked No. 8 in the USTA boys 16's in 1956, just behind such legends as Butch Buchholz and Donald Dell. He graduated from Georgia Tech in 1960, and was inducted into the Georgia Tech Athletic hall of fame in 1969.

He played Wimbledon twice, the Australian Open once, the French Open once, and the U. S. Open seven times, reaching the third round in 1963 when he was defeated by Butch Bucholz.

He was later president of the Georgia Tennis Foundation and inducted into the Georgia Tennis and the International Tennis Halls of Fame.

He was killed in August 1999 when his private plane overshot a slippery rain-soaked runway in Florida. He placed his daughter Emma behind him, and she survived.

Ned Neely, right, with Georgia Tech Coach Bortell, 1960

ROBERT LEE DODD
1908-1988

After a spectacular career in football, both as a player (University of Tennessee Football Hall of Fame) and a coach (Georgia Tech, 165-64-8 , 22 years, a 31 game winning streak from 1951–1952, two SEC titles and the College Football Hall of Fame as a coach), Bobby Dodd proved he could make it happen with a tennis racket.

How can an aging ex-football coach with near non-existent tennis strokes even get on the court with top level players, much less win tournament after tournament, many of them state championships, in age divisions with players less than half his age? Because, as Cole Porter once said, *"...you got that thing, that certain thing..."* He had it. The thing was lightning quick reflexes and extraordinary hand-eye coordination.

The tennis stories about him are legend. His unorthodox style someone once described as looking like a person falling out of a tree. But he was a fabulous doubles partner. He covered the court well despite his age, and played "within himself," never trying things beyond his ability, and his best shot was a protective one, which his friends called the "shovel shot," a monster lob often so high that his opponents were forced to hit overheads on vertically descending balls, not easy for even an expert to do.

He played many memorable matches with Atlanta pro Joe Becknell as his partner. One time when two young girls who had just won the U.S. Open doubles at Forest Hills came to Atlanta, someone arranged a match for them against Dodd and Becknell. Joe was twice as old, Dodd three times as old, as the two champions, but Dodd and Becknell won the first set and at one point had them on the ropes in the second set, an ace away from winning.

COURTESY SOUTHERN TENNIS ASSOCIATION

Youth and agility eventually prevailed, but it was a match talked about for years.

He was a regular at Bitsy Grant Tennis Center, playing mostly with Bitsy Grant, Tom Bird, and Hank Crawford, always on court one.

An observer recalled once seeing the four walk out on court one when a group was in the midst of a match. The group asked, *"what are you doing?"* The terse reply: *"we're playing here."* Without further ado, Grant and crew commenced their normal warmup, all eight of them then on the court. One of the group walked up the steps to complain. Whoever was on duty told them, *"...no, you don't understand. The place is named for him. And he plays on court one. Whenever he wants. You'll have to move."*

And that was the end of that. And after tennis, it was usually checkers, the post-match game of choice.

"Our most memorable match ever was during the 1977 Georgia State Championships, Men's' 35's doubles. I was 39, and Big Coach (my nickname for Dodd) was 68. We won it, 1-6, 6-4, 6-4 . It wasn't the first victory we had playing together, but the sweetest.

"The No. 1 seeded team was John Skogstad & Harry Thompson, the best doubles team in the southeast in prior years age divisions and now in the 35's. Big Coach & I had never beaten Skog and Harry. We had played them some good matches where we won a set now and then, but they were just too good. In this particular tournament, Skog and Harry were upset in the semi-finals by Speed Howell and Rod Carlyle...

"That particular August day, the temperature was about 95 degrees with high humidity, brutal conditions for all of us. Another thing that made this match special was that both Speed and Rod were in their mid 30's. We were giving up a lot of years. We started, and the match went badly the first set, and quick, 20 minutes. Speed and Rod were eating our lobs alive, blasting over-heads from everywhere and not missing any.

"I asked Coach what we should do, and he said, 'we're not changing anything. If they play that good for the whole match, they're going to win, and deserve it. But I don't think they can.' They didn't. A few overhead misses here and there, a few unforced errors, and they were back down to earth. We won a close second set, 6-4, and somehow got up a break in the third set, and got a match point. Coach threw up one of his shovel shot lobs, but it fell far short, barely past the service line, which may have thrown Speed off a little, because he blew his overhead long, and we won the match.

"I was whipped, and so were Speed and Rod, in those conditions. We all three limped off the court. But the Coach was strutting around fresh as a daisy. He said later that this win was the greatest athletic achievement of his life. Pretty impressive when one considers his remarkable football career, both playing and coaching."

Joe Becknell, 2009

COURTESY JOE BECKNELL

The Dodd strut

"I last saw the coach in the locker room at Bitsy, in the mid '80's, then aging, but with that twinkle still in his eye.

"My strongest recollection of him goes back to the '50's when I was a student, at Grant Field, my date and I watching Tech play football, Dodd in coat and tie and his lucky brown hat, pacing back and forth with a formality that spoke volumes. In all those years at Tech he never had a contract. Just a handshake.

"He's oft quoted saying, '...most of my players graduated. I told their parents, when I was recruiting, send me your boy and I'll send him back a better man.' I doubt he ever failed to deliver on that promise.

"I watched he and Becknell play that match in 1977, and I still can't believe what I saw."

Author, 2010

DEWITT REDGRAVE, JR.
1899-1998

He began playing tennis at age 24, self taught, as a young naval officer, after watching play at the Longwood Cricket Club while attending nearby MIT. He later read Bill Tilden's books, "Match Play" and "Spin of the Ball".

He improved quickly, and was a member of the Navy's Leech Club team from 1926 to 1937 in its annual competition against Army. Tilden remained a tennis hero for him and he actually played against Tilden socially during WW II while stationed in Philadelphia. Later he had an opportunity to hit with Maureen Connolly, immediately dubbing her a "future U.S. Singles Champion". She was, three years later.

He did not reach national prominence as a player until after his retirement from the Navy in 1950 when he began a new career as vice President of Research at Georgia. Tech. He had umpired at the U.S. Championships at Forest Hills for 17 years and had a strong interest in the game.

In 1952 he won the Georgia State 45's Singles title, at age 53.

He was later instrumental in establishing the USTA Super Senior division for players over 70. He went on to win eight USTA National titles, on all four surfaces, four in singles and four in doubles, two each with partners Gordon Steele and Stephen Graves.

In 1980 he was ranked nationally No. 1 in Men's 80 Singles and No 4 in doubles.

An avid spectator as well as player, he attended Wimbledon over 20 times, Roland Garros over 10 times, and watched many epic court battles, including Don Budge's comeback victory in Davis Cup competition over Baron Gottfried von Cramm in 1937.

COURTESY SOUTHERN TENNIS ASSOCIATION

He was a frequent visitor to and player at Bitsy Grant Tennis Center, until age 95. He was predeceased by his son DeWitt III, who for years served as Executive Director of the Southern Tennis Association and was noted particularly for his work in junior tennis development. Under his direction, the STA membership grew to over 60,000.

" Capt Redgrave was a contemporary and friend of my father. I remember running into him, by chance, at \the U.S. Open in Forest Hills in the 60's, both of us watching early round play on a field court. He had a small notebook and was making an entry on what seemed every point. Our conversation was brief; his mind was on his note-taking, possibly of a potential opponent. The episode exemplified his analytical approach to the game."

Author, 2009

CAROLYN SHERMAN HOWELL

"The Howells won many Atlanta City, Georgia State and Southern tennis titles in singles, doubles, mixed doubles, father-son, and mother-daughter events. In the Crackerland tournament in Athens it was not unusual for all eight Howells to be playing on our courts simultaneously. It was a surprise to no one when the Howells were named the Southern Tennis Association's Family of the Year in 1965.

"My son Ham was so used to seeing Carrie in her tennis outfit that once when he saw her at a social gathering, he commented later to me: 'Mrs. Howell was at a wedding party one night and was all dressed up. I hardly recognized her with all her clothes on.' "

Dan Magill, 2009

Carrie Howell

Carrie taught herself to play tennis by reading a book by Rene' LaCoste, *"LaCoste on Tennis," (1928),* now a collectors item. She became an accomplished player and was inducted into the Georgia Tennis Hall of Fame. She passed on her knowledge and passion for the game to her six children. The family tennis academy was the backyard court.

She was hard to miss; she was always in her "uniform," white shorts and sleeveless white blouse, and a (now legendary, still mysterious) thermos of iced tea. It apparently had magical powers because she seldom lost a match.

FRANK WILLETT

He won the National Boys Indoor in 1940. Playing for Georgia Tech under Coach Earl Bortell, he reached the semis of the National NCAA singes in 1945, losing to eventual winner and later touring pro Pancho Segura of University of Miami.

He had won the Alabama High School Athletic Association singles in 1941 and 1942, and later won numerous Georgia and Southern Open titles. He was ranked No. 1 in the Southern doubles 6 times. He was inducted into the Southern Tennis Hall of Fame in 1987 and the Georgia Tech Athletics Hall of Fame, 1961.

Frank Willett, 1957, after winning the Southern Open Singles in New Orleans, LA

HERMAN L. RATCLIFF
1910-2001

"I tried golf, but it was making me fat..."

Anyone who looks will see that in the senior age divisions, the USTA Yearbook is riddled with the name "Ratcliffe". Before it was over, he had won 23 national titles. Herman was the first Georgian ever to win a "grand slam" of national titles, indoor, hard, grass and clay, by winning the 80's doubles with partner Vince Connerat. He did it three times, once in the 80's and twice in the 85's.

His story is amazing in several ways. For one, he never lifted a racket until he was 65. He retired and learned the game on his own, and because his resources were limited, when he played in tournaments, he literally slept in his car, to avoid hotel expense. Not only that, he ate in, meaning, in his case, just outside his car, which was an aging panel truck, that he referred to as his "van."

The second amazing thing is where he came from. It was a place with no tennis courts, in Atlanta's Bellwood section. His family lived in a house with no electricity, no plumbing, no phone, and you bathed in a washtub. His father was a flagman on the Atlanta/Birmingham/Nashville RR.

Herman always worked during school, delivering ice from a horse drawn wagon, throwing two paper routes, and selling newspapers in the old Peachtree Arcade building, making a penny per paper.

After graduating from high school he went to work for the Southern Wax Paper Company, working 80 hours a week, paid on a "piecework" basis, sometimes making as much as thirty dollars (*"I was a fast wrapper"*). College was never on his radar.

He recalls one of the high points of his early working days with Southern Wax Paper was

AUGUST 9, 1990. ATLANTA JOURNAL-CONSTITUTION, WITH PERMISSION. COPYRIGHT, ALL RIGHTS RESERVED

Copyright Atlanta Journal-Constitution. Courtesy of Georgia State University.

being promoted from "wrapper" (of candy, dinner rolls, and other food items) to "bookkeeper." He had taken an accounting course in high school. His pay went from $30/week, his average for piece work, to $15/week. But he stayed with the company for 41 years, retiring in the 1970's, then making $1200/month. A pittance by the standards of most; to him, it was *"a small fortune."*

He had tried golf after retiring, but said *"...it was making me fat..."* and decided to try tennis. His beginnings at Bitsy Grant Tennis Center weren't encouraging; *"... I didn't win a single match..."* but he stayed with it, being allowed occasionally to play with Grant and his buddies.

He drove his van all over the contiguous U.S., West Coast included, more than once, mostly buying only gas, groceries, and propane. *"...It's just fine, I built a bed frame out of 2X4's, Nell and I sleep on that, we have a cooler and a hot plate, and some folding chairs..."*

"Oh yeah, I don't just want to win, I want to tear somebody up if I can…

I don't mean I'd hurt 'em, of course

"I first ran into Herman at a tournament yeas ago in LaGrange, Georgia, both of us sitting on some wooden stands, I having just finished a first round match in the 45's, he having done the same in the 65's, and we have a 30 minute talk ("call me Bubba") and he tells me the part about just taking up the game.

"I'm not impressed. He doesn't look like a tennis player. Small in stature, he looks like he's missed a lot of meals, and probably doesn't tip the scales at much over 100 pounds.

"I forgot it. Then 15 years later, I'm idly thumbing through the pages of a tennis magazine, and see an article headlined 'Herman Ratcliffe defeats Gardner Mulloy in 75's Grass in Hartford CT…' It has a picture. Holy cow, this is the guy I talked to years ago. Mulloy had been a world top ten player. How could this happen? It did. The article went on to describe Ratcliff's vaulting over the net at the conclusion of the match, saying, '…better luck next time…'

"Years later I asked him about that match, and about playing on grass. He told me he learned quick how to play on it. 'What's that'? I said. His quick reply, '…don't' let the ball bounce…' He was quick enough to do it."

Author, 2011

Later there were tournaments he couldn't drive to, like those in Europe, when he played as a team member representing the U.S. in Bitsy Grant Cup and Talbert Cup international competition. Somehow he managed, thanks to Las Vegas billionaire Kirk Kerkorian and other sponsors.

The Los Angeles Times, in June 1998, covered Portschach, an event in Austria in which thirteen accomplished U.S. senior men players, all over 85, went to Austria for an unusual event for "*really old people,*" as one of them quipped, their expenses partly defrayed by Kerkorian.

They played alongside competitors in the first-ever international team event for women 75-and-over. A reporter covering the event observed:

"*…Take Herman "Bubba" Ratcliffe., a former Georgia paper mill manager with 19 national… titles to his credit. He wears a hearing aid and weighs 135 pounds, but you don't mess with Bubba. Angered by his Romanian opponent's call in this umpire-less competition, he raced across the clay court and wagged a finger in his face: 'I get another serve!' He won his way, if not the match.* "

"*Oh yeah, I don't just want to win, I want to tear somebody up if I can,*" he deadpanned; afterward, saying, "*I don't mean I'd hurt 'em, of course.*"

He enjoyed phenomenal health most of his life; Nell fell victim to the ravages of age, suffering for years with high blood pressure and heart disease. But she traveled with him to tournaments in the van. He did all the cleaning, cooking, and washing when she became unable. He loved life.

"*I love the game, I love the guys I play with, even the ones who cheat. Its always a thrill for me.*"

He married Nell in 1936 after meeting her at a West End Woman's Club dance. They lived in the same small house in Hapeville, Georgia. for the next 50 years.

Only a lucky handful have a stash of memories like Bubba's.

DAN MAGILL

Tennis in Georgia has been shaped and molded over the last hundred years by a legion of people, places and events, but none of them could be more than a distant second to what has been done for the game by Daniel Hamilton Magill.

The tennis part of his life began, as a seven year old at the Athens YMCA camp[1], when he first observed Vince Connerat, who was *"keeping up the courts"* (sic), playing with Dr. Frank Kelles Boland, the camp physician.

In the years to come he was into other activities; varsity swimming for the University of Georgia; assistant to legendary football coach Harry Mehre; a Marine Captain in WWII; sports writing; promotion of the Georgia high school All-Star games; University of Georgia assistant swimming coach; radio and television appearances; and the promotion, fundraising and construction of the Collegiate Tennis Hall of Fame (donated by country music legend Kenny Rogers); and, in 1954, coach to a struggling University of Georgia tennis team, a position he took temporarily while looking for a permanent coach, but would hold for the next 34 years, amassing an amazing 706-183 record (second most wins by any coach in history after former Stanford Coach Dick Gould).

He molded UGA tennis into a powerhouse; 13 Conference outdoor championships, 8 SEC indoor championships, and 2 NCAA championships. His 1985 Bulldogs performed the unmatched *"hat trick"* (sic) - they ranked No. 1 in the final national team rankings, No. 1 in individual singles (Mikael Pernfors), and No. 1 in doubles (Mikael Pernfors and Allen Miller.) Along the way, he built, bit by bit, UGA's tennis complex, considered by many to be the finest in the country, and brought the ITA Collegiate Tennis Hall of Fame to Athens.

COLLEGIATE TENNIS HALL OF FAME

Dan Magill in his office in the Collegiate Tennis Hall of Fame, Athens, Georgia

The complex of courts and tennis buildings at the University of Georgia is named in his honor.

Upon meeting him, one senses a man who is bent on making the most out of not just every minute, but every second, of his life. Tall and imposing, with an elocution honed through years of public speaking, one gets the feeling that his mind is several steps ahead in the conversation. And it is. After talking a few minutes, one can glimpse what makes him tick; a fascination with athletics (a youth spent swimming and playing tennis, baseball, basketball, and ping pong); a drive for involvement and personal athletic achievement (varsity tennis and swimming at UGA); and an amazing recall of sports minutia.

Couple those with exceptional writing and speaking talent (BA Journalism, UGA, a lifetime of writing for the Atlanta Journal and the Athens Banner Herald), all in a state of perpetual simultaneous motion, as in watching a six ring circus with different acts going on all at one time, and you have some sense of the man.

[1] *The Athens Y Camp for Boys is located in the mountains of North Georgia.*

The UGA courts, under Magill leadership, were also the venue for many years for the "GIAA" (Georgia Interscholastic Athletic Association) tournament, the culmination of the year for high school tennis players in the state.

And tennis is now, after near eighty years of involvement in other sports, a major focus of his life. He plays three times a week, and is Curator of the Collegiate Tennis Hall of Fame Museum. But not the only one. He walks two miles every morning and makes countless speeches and public appearances.

He began his 59-year association with University of Georgia athletics as a baseball bat-boy in the 1930's and continued in numerous roles until his retirement in 1995. *"I don't know of anyone who has contributed more to our program through his time, his commitment, his life," said UGA athletic director Vince Dooley. "He, more than anyone else, has always been the true Bulldog spirit of the Georgia people."*

Magill retired as head tennis coach following the 1988 season after leading the Bulldogs for 34 years and becoming one of the most influential men in the history of collegiate tennis. He remained on the University's athletic staff through 1995 as Director of Men's and Women's Tennis as well as Assistant Athletic Director for Public Relations.

During his long tenure with the University, he also served 27 years as sports information director and 25 years as secretary of the Georgia Bulldog Club, which he founded in 1953. He was inducted into the UGA Circle of Honor - the pinnacle of recognition for former coaches and athletes at Georgia - and was a recipient of the Bill Hartman Award which goes annually to a former athlete or coach who has made a significant impact in his chosen career. He's also a member of the National Collegiate Tennis Hall of Fame, State of Georgia Sports Hall of Fame, and Southern Tennis Hall of Fame.

UGA student Magill working the chains

Perhaps one of the greatest testaments to Magill's contribution to UGA is that today nearly 50 people do the jobs that he once did on his own. His passion for the school continues even today as he personally gives tours of the Collegiate Tennis Hall of Fame.

In 1982, UGA benefactor Lindsey Hopkins, Jr., a major stockholder in the Coca-Cola Company, prevailed on Magill to spend several weeks in China, teaching Chinese pros how to teach tennis. The trip was partially sponsored by Coke. He remarked at one point, innocently to his beautiful interpreter, Li Li, that he could not tell the difference between a Chinese, a Japanese, or a Vietnamese person. Her quick response was, with an engaging smile, that she could not tell the difference between a *"monkee, donkee, or Yankee."* Magill's feeble effort to recover from this conversational trumping, that he was from the southern part of the U.S. and therefore not a *"yankee,"* was lost on the victorious Li Li.

Magill officially retired from the University in 1995, leaving behind a legacy like no other. In his honor, the press box at Georgia's Sanford Stadium was named for him during a ceremony prior to the Oct. 23 1999 game between the Bulldogs and Kentucky, and a plaque with his biography is mounted alongside other Bulldog greats. His seat assignment in the press box reads, "Dan Magill - Legend."

He is.

His mark was not left only on tennis. His amazing energy and creativity touched all collegiate sports. He changed, almost single-handedly, a lethargic UGA fan base into what is now an unstoppable behemoth of team spirit. Writer Gene Asher (*"Legends-Georgians Who Lived Impossible Dreams")* described what Magill found upon arriving at UGA: *"...you could have fired a howitzer in Sanford Stadium in 1950 at some (football) games and not hit anyone..."*

Enter Magill, and what happened in the next few years was his single handed crusade to rectify the situation. Traveling the state from one end to the other, he conceived the idea of "Bulldog Clubs" and managed to start one in almost every Georgia town, often bringing with him Coach Wally Butts and a few of the football players. The result of the effort is evidenced today by sellouts in every sport, cars heading for games with Bulldog flags flying, filled up hotels and loud, woofing fans, even at tennis matches. So much so that rival NCAA tennis coaches would complain that Georgia had an unfair advantage in Athens, and was virtually unbeatable there.

His flair for promotion started early on. One incident described in detail in his book *"Match Pointers"* tells it all. It was his staging of the "great snake fight", on the UGA varsity tennis courts in the 1930's, pitting his captured king snake against a friend's timber rattler.

Magill had caught his at the girl's Athens Y camp in Oconee County; the friend had picked up his rattler at the Athens Y camp for boys in Rabun county.

The event was hyped, tickets sold, 10 cents each, and an article appeared in the Athens Banner Herald spreading the word (Magill's father was editor at the time). When the bell rang, neither snake seemed interested in anything more than a nap. The large crowd became restless, and after murmurs of a refund, Magill, in an attempt to save the day, taunted the rattler, causing him to strike at him, luckily missing, but the audience was placated. The event ended with both snakes going back to taking a nap. Since they seemed friendly to each other, the boys decided to house them together in the same cage.

Things went well for several weeks, until one day the rattler was missing from the cage, and the king snake was somewhat fatter, Magill noting that *"...he had a satisfied smile on his face."*

A dog is named for him. Uga VI (pronounced "ugah"), Georgia's perennial mascot, carried the official name of "Uga Magillicuddy" in honor of Magill. The bulldog was featured on the cover of Sports Illustrated 1997 and was named the best mascot in college sports in the same publication. Uga V had previously fallen into disgrace, and garnered national attention when he lunged at football player Robert Baker in a four-overtime Georgia victory in 1996.[1]

[1]*Sonny Seiler, a Savannah Georgia attorney, loyal alum (and erstwhile bit part movie actor, in the film adaptation of "Midnight in the Garden of Good and Evil", filmed in part in Savannah) has bred an unbroken line of bulldogs, all pure white, as UGA mascots since the 1950's. The first one appeared in September 1956 in Sanford Stadium at a Florida State-UGA game, with Seiler, and their picture appeared in Atlanta and Athens papers. Magill, the UGA Sports Information Director at the time, noticed, and suggested to then coach Wally Butts that he appear at all the games as the official team mascot. The tradition has endured now for over 50 years.*

> *"I was never in the match from that point on…"*

"Early in my career I lost a big junior match when my opponent utilized the drop shot to lure me to the net to take advantage of my practically nonexistent volley and overhead. I was a classic victim of the drop shot that day. The match happened to be in the state junior tournament in Atlanta in the late 1930's. My opponent was the reigning Southern Boys' 18 champion, Cortez Suttles of East Point.

" I was winning most of the points in long baseline rallies on the slow red clay courts, which caused Cortez' coach, Bill Lufler (the first teaching pro in Atlanta, I believe) to send instructions to his protégé' to use the drop shot to bring me to the net and then either to pass or lob over me. This tactic worked to perfection. Even when I had a chance to volley, I would hit a set-up, and I messed up numerous times with my overhead errors. I was never in the match from that point on. …I did profit by that hard lesson…it's no problem if you get to the drop shots in plenty of time; then you can win the point with a variety of shots. …

"I never once thought about developing a drop shot myself until I was in my late thirties, playing state champion Don Floyd…in the Georgia State Men's Open in the late 1950's on clay at the Bitsy Grant Tennis Center in Atlanta. It was a semifinal match and Don prevailed, 6-4, 6-4.

After this match, Don gave me some good advice: 'Dan, I've been watching you play a number of years, and you don't have a single shot with which you can earn the point. 'You're just hoping to out steady your opponent. You need a shot that will end the point in your favor, and I recommend that you work on the drop shot, which can easily be developed off a chop stroke—just the kind you use off both sides…'

"I went back to Athens and experimented with the drop shot, and, sure enough, it was easy for me…it was natural with my chop-stroke style. …the drop shot has become my best shot and has helped me win some state and Southern senior titles.

"Some years ago there was a poll among players, ranking the bet shot makers in the South, and I won in the drop shot category. The great Billie Jean King heard about this when she visited her brother Randy Moffitt…in Athens… in 1993. I arranged a doubles match for Billie Jean at our indoor courts. She and former Georgia player Jack Frierson played several sets against Georgia women's coach Jeff Wallace and former Georgia NCAA doubles champion Allen Miller, following which I told Billie Jean that she had the best volleying form I had ever seen, man or woman.

"As I was getting ready to leave, Allen Miller said, 'hey coach, Billie Jean wants to see your dreaded drop shot'. I knew she was teasing, but I grabbed a racket, Coach Wallace fed me a ball, and I hit a perfect one, first forehand, then backhand. She laughed, and said, 'Fantastic! Best I ever saw!'

Dan Magill, *"Match pointers"*

Magill was inducted into the Georgia Sports Hall of Fame in 1976. In his spare time (?), he manages to tend 1000 or so azaleas in the landscape of his Athens home and play a rigorous tournament schedule, consistently maintaining a high ranking in his age group.

RUTH RYNER LAY

How does one learn to play tennis in Vienna, Georgia? Less than 1000 families live there. The only answer is, be born with natural talent. Vienna's main attractions are the one stop light, the Georgia Cotton Museum, and the Big Pig Jig, reputed to be one of the state's best barbecue restaurants.

Lay was a top junior tennis player in high school, and graduated from Agnes Scott College with a major in psychology.

After college Lay continued to play competitive tennis and won numerous championships throughout the South, including the North Carolina Invitational, the Atlanta City Open, the Georgia State Open, and the Crackerland in Athens, Ga.

She later became involved in coaching top junior players, including some who joined the pro tour. She's always devoted her time unselfishly as a volunteer to the sport.

She was instrumental in organizing an early form of league play in the 1960s in which five Atlanta clubs were involved, in a women's interclub competition: Bitsy Grant Tennis Center, Brookhaven, Cherokee Town Club, East Lake Country Club and the Piedmont Driving Club. She later shared her experience with Charlie Cox, the 1971 president of the Atlanta Lawn Tennis Association, which led to the league play we know today as ALTA.

She has been secretary/treasurer of the Southern Tennis Association, active in the USTA as coach of the girl's Intersectional team, Chairwoman of the STA Women's and Girls Advisory Committee, a member of the USTA membership and international play committees, and chair of the Junior Wightman Cup Committee.

Ruth Lay, left, at conclusion of a match with Mary Ann Connerat, right

She was successful in tournament play, winning many state and Southern titles in many age divisions. She received the STA Jacob's Bowl award and was inducted into the Georgia Tennis Hall of Fame in 1982, followed by the Southern Tennis Hall of Fame, the USTA Service Bowl, and International Who's Who of Tennis.

A USPTA Professional, she was for years the Tennis Director at North Park Tennis Center in Alpharetta, Georgia. She previously was a tennis professional at World Championship Tennis (now called the Racket Club of the South), Horseshoe Bend Country Club and Cross Creek Tennis Club. She is a member of the USTA Olympic and Maureen Connolly Brinker Cup committees. Forty four of the players she coached won college scholarships, and four competed in the French Open, Australian Open, and other international events.

In 1992 she was recognized by the USTA for her 25 years of volunteer service by president Bob Cookson at the annual meeting. Her efforts date back to the 50's when she began playing tournaments in Atlanta and became involved with ALTA and the GTA as a tournament director and junior tennis promoter.

CRAWFORD HENRY

COURTESY GEORGIA TENNIS HALL OF FAME

Crawford grew up playing near downtown Atlanta, at the old Northside Tennis Club on Argonne Ave., near Peachtree St. He was taught early on by his uncle, Don Smith, who lived close by.

He was virtually unbeatable in high school, playing for Grady; he won four state high school championships. His high school coach was the legendary Erk Russell[1]. He also won the U.S. Interscholastic singles championship in 1955.

He was on the U.S. National Junior Davis Cup Team, losing his first match to Ken Rosewall. He went on to play for Tulane, and was the first Georgian to win an NCAA singles title. He won the NCAA doubles with Ron Holmberg in '57 and '59. He played the international circuit for five years, long before there was any real money in it, with wins over Arthur Ashe, Roy Emerson, Donald Dell, Frank Froeling, Marty Riesen, and Orlando Sepeda. At one point he held a US ranking of No. 10 in singles and No. 4 in doubles.

He later began a career in college coaching, first with Oglethorpe University, where his record in 1963 was 16-0, the team's only undefeated season, and then at Emory, where he compiled a 51-23 record in four years. He left college coaching in the 60's, and helped design DeKalb Tennis Center, where he was the tennis director for 10 years.

He returned to college coaching for his alma mater, Tulane University, where in three years he compiled a 42-29 record. He returned to Atlanta to become director of tennis at Chattahoochee Plantation Club. While there, he worked with Allen Miller, who became an NCAA champion and nationally ranked player. In 1983, he returned to college coaching, at North Carolina State, where he stayed for 13 years. He is in the Georgia Tennis, Southern Tennis and Tulane University Sports Halls of Fame. Retired in Atlanta, he now plays golf every day (according to daughter Laura).

[1] *Erk Russell is best known in football circles, but had tennis credentials. He played varsity tennis at Auburn, and was the school's last four sport letterman, earning 10 varsity letters while there. He was Georgia's defensive coordinator for 17 years, then brought a dormant Georgia Southern football team to three NCAA Div. I-AA championships as head coach.*

PIERRE HOWARD JR.

"Pierre" is a rather unusual name in the deep South. But then Pierre Howard Jr. is a rather unusual person. Anyone who navigates the gauntlet of career politics and comes out in one piece has to be unusual, in a smart sort of way. He did, successfully, beginning as a State Representative in the 1970's and serving there for 17 years, then being elected Lt. Governor of Georgia in 1990, serving two consecutive terms.

A standout on the University of Georgia's tennis team in the 1960's, he has remained close to Coach Dan Magill for many years. Magill observed to him once that "Pierre" might be difficult for the average Georgia voter to swallow; and suggested he work on a way to fix it. Pierre turned it into an advantage, often starting speeches with the explanation that "Pierre" means "Bubba" in French. It went so far that the head of the University's French Department, Dr. Jean-Pierre Piriou, began receiving letters addressed to "Dr. Bubba Piriou." Their friendship has endured. Howard's fluency in French didn't hurt.

The Magill/Howard relationship was always marked with humorous sparring. Once, anticipating that Pierre would be almost certain to show off his newly awarded Phi Beta Kappa key at practice, Magill borrowed his wife Rosemary's, and sure enough, there was a "key-off."

"Why I do declare, Pierre, your key is the same design as the one I got back in 1942..."

Caught off guard, Howard stammered *"why Coach, I never knew you made Phi Beta Kappa!"* To which Magill modestly replied, *"well, its no big deal - - I don't make a habit of flaunting it in front of my less intelligent friends..."* Magill 1, Howard 0. A little research, and the ruse was exposed for all the team to see, and Pierre had the last laugh.

He once set up Magill by asking him to demonstrate his famous fingertip chinning trick, on the door sill in his office, to a "friend". The pair had secretly greased the door sill with vaseline. All went well until Magill gave his "customary finishing flourish" by kicking both feet out, which landed him on the floor with a concussion and a trip to the ER at Athens General Hospital. Pierre was victorious, but with a close call. After graduation he earned a law degree from the University of Georgia.

One would never guess his impressive political lineage nor his political achievements. He never mentioned them, and most times his tennis companions hadn't a clue. His great-grandfather Thomas Coke Howard was a member of the Georgia House of Representatives, and his grandfather, William Schley Howard, a noted Georgia attorney, served in both the Georgia House and the U.S. House of Representatives. His father Pierre Sr. was a well known Atlanta attorney.

Pierre was more than competent on the court, and was awarded a tennis scholarship to the University of Georgia. He had won the Atlanta Boys' 16 singles while a student at Decatur High. He and Bob Hardcastle, later a star at Tulane, were ranked No. 1 in doubles in the Southern 18's in 1960. Pierre's father, Pierre Sr., had played No. 1 singles at Emory years before.

According to Magill, Pierre's most difficult match was against a girl. Roberta Allison[1], 19, was on the Alabama roster in 1963, just after the SEC decision to allow females to play on heretofore all male teams, when most colleges had little more than intramural programs for women students. Georgia's Becky Birchmore had stunned her male Auburn opponent a month before, when the Georgia Mens' team played them; now the tables were turned, and Pierre drew the short straw, at No. 4 singles.

To make matters worse, it was played in Tuscaloosa, with a large, noisy partisan crowd of students watching, shouting taunts like, *"hey lard butt, you're gonna get beat by a girl today..."* and similar insults. Magill said later he had selected Howard for the task because he knew he could keep his cool better than most of the other players. After a 2 hour duel, he prevailed, giving Roberta her first loss of the season, and amazingly received a standing ovation from the 'Bama fans. He wasn't a lard butt when it started, and he was anything but when it concluded, barely winning the first set 7-5, and having lost 10 pounds when it was all over.

With movie star Kim Basinger, at the occasion of turning on the lights at the Dan Magill Tennis Complex, which she funded.

"Pierre's tennis during his working years was most often at the public DeKalb Tennis Center. Back then, in the 70's and through the 90's, DeKalb was a 'show up and find a game' place.

"A lot of us had uncertain schedules, you came if you could, and almost always you could find a game. Pierre's level was considerably above most of us, but he happily played with whomever was there.

"Most players made the concession to style when tennis clothes began to come in all colors, but Pierre was always in traditional white, both shirt and shorts.

"His court demeanor was impeccable. He would never stoop to questioning a line call, but you knew if he thought your call was bad, because you got The Look. He was just a plain guy but with style, elegance, polish and class.

"Our fathers were tennis companions. My dad told me that Pierre Sr.'s wife once told him, "I can always tell if Pierre won as soon as he walks in the door. If he lost, he's not whistling."

Author, 2011

[1] *Allison had been recruited by Alabama's men's tennis coach Jason Morton when he discovered her practicing for the U.S. Championships on a private grass court in Tuscaloosa. She played at No. 4 her first year, then was moved to No. 1. Some schools defaulted to her rather than risk a loss to a woman. She won the women's' collegiate singles in '62 and '63, and was inducted into the Southern Lawn Tennis and the Alabama Tennis Halls of Fame, and played several years on the Women's' Tour.*

DONNA FLOYD FALES

COURTESY DONNA FLOYD FALES

Her father Don related in an interview once that his daughter's tennis career started at Northside Tennis Club in Atlanta, when, at 11 months, she would play with tennis balls rolled to her. Quite a leap from there to becoming the U.S. Women's Clay Court Champion (right). It was no accident. She got her first racket at age 5, and played her first tournament match, the Atlanta City Championships, in the open division in 1951, drawing a seeded player in the first round. After dropping the first set 6-0, she came back to win the match. She was eliminated by a top high school player in the second round, but the stage was set. In the years following she would spend at least three hours a day on the court.

Donna Floyd Fales
1960 U.S. Women's Open Clay

Tennis wasn't her total sports activity. At Moreland Elementary School, she played volleyball and basketball, once racking up 28 points in a basketball game after father Don offered her a nickel for every point she scored. Her dad observed later, "*I never made the nickel offer again. Too expensive.*" The Moreland volleyball team won the Atlanta City Parks and Recreation championship two years running. Mother Evelyn: "*...she's a perfectionist; she comes home at night and practices her swing in front of a mirror.*"

In the years between 1960 and 1976, she won, in addition to the U.S. Open Clay, the U.S. National Collegiate Singles and the U.S. Open Mixed Doubles; and was ranked in the top ten nationally for six years, reaching a career high of 5 in 1960 and 1962. In the same period she played on and captained both the Wightman Cup and Federation Cup teams. She had been first selected for the Southern Junior Wightman Cup team in 1953 at age 12, the youngest player ever.

COURTESY DONNA FLOYD FALES

Donna Floyd played her first tournament at age 10 in 1951, the Atlanta City Championships. Pictured above, with father Donald

Years later she played team tennis for the Florida Flamingos, with team mates Frank Froeling, Cliff Drysdale, and Mark Cox; and Bueno Cup, as captain and player. She reached the quarters of the U.S. Open, Wimbledon, and the French Championships.

In 2005, she captured the U.S. Women's National 60's Grass singles and doubles, and the International Tennis Federation World Super Senior Individual Singles; and in 2008 the U.S. Women's National Grass (open division) Doubles.

Between playing, she's been a tennis commentator with Bud Collins; run a large tennis facility at the Kings Bay Resort in Miami; developed and directed adult tennis clinics and junior camps at the Sheraton Royal Biscayne; coordinated and orchestrated two Pringles Light pro-celebrity tournaments for the WTA; and served on the coaching staff of the University of Miami Women's Tennis team.

More recently she's founded and served as President of the Greater Miami Tennis Patrons Foundation. She's served as Tournament Director for the Orange Bowl International Tennis Championship and the ITF Sunshine and Connolly Cup Championships.

Donna Floyd Fales
At William and Mary College

She's served on the boards and committees of numerous tennis related organizations, including the USTA's committees for Women's Senior International Play, Fed Cup, ITF Hall of Fame Awards (chair), Amateur Rules, Minority Participation, and Grievance; as CEO and President, National Junior Tennis League; Director Royal Palm Tennis Club; director of tennis at the Riviera Country Club; director WPBT/channel 2; Board of Trustees and Executive Committee, Ransom Everglades School, Coconut Grove, FL; Chair of the tennis subcommittee, Miami Sports Authority; and the Junior League of Miami.

As one might expect, numerous awards have come her way: the USTA Service Bowl Award; the USTA Community Service Award; the Sarah Palfrey Danzig Award of the United States International Club; the Babe Didrikson Zaharias Award; the International Tennis Hall of Fame Educational Merit Award; the USTA Volunteer Service Award (45 years); the William and Mary Athletic Hall of Fame Award; the National Capital Area Tennis Hall of Fame; the Florida Tennis Hall of Fame; the Dade County Tennis Hall of Fame; the Virginia Sports Hall of Fame; the Women's Collegiate Tennis Hall of Fame; the Arlington County Sports Hall of Fame; the Wakefield High School Hall of Fame; and the Greater Miami Chamber of Commerce Lifetime Contributions to Sports Award.

Her community service has not been limited to tennis; she currently serves (in 2011) as the Executive Director of Rebuilding Together Miami-Dade, Inc.

And she's still playing, at a world class level. The fall of 2009 found her in Perth, Australia, at the Alexander Park Tennis Club, playing Kitty Godfree Cup (65+) matches on grass against France, Switzerland, and other teams from around the world. And winning.

ALLEN MORRIS

Allen Morris grew up on Penn Avenue, in what is now downtown Atlanta. Tall, muscular and athletic, he could have been successful in any sport. His path to tennis swung on two life changing events, without which he might now be in other sports record books.

The first was at age 12, when Don Smith (uncle of Georgia Tennis HOF member Crawford Henry), a neighbor several years older, introduced him to tennis. He lived next door, and was in the habit of cutting through the Morris family yard on his way to the four clay courts of the Atlanta Tennis Club on Argonne Avenue, two blocks away, often just to hit on the backboard there after school. Allen followed him one day, and at Don's invitation, picked up a tennis racket and hit a few balls. Afterwards Don worked with him often. When it rained and the courts were unplayable (drying of Georgia red clay courts often took several days) they hit balls in the street.

For his 13th birthday, his father surprised him with a bargain counter Sears Roebuck racket, $1.49 (according to Jim Minter, Atlanta Journal, in 1956). He became a fixture around the courts, hitting balls with anyone he could, and getting to know most of the members. Dr. Ralph Aiken, a member, having gotten a new racket, tossed Allen his old one, a Spalding, much better than the Sears one. The club then hired him to maintain the courts. With encouragement from some of the members, he began to enter tournaments, and at age 15, won the Atlanta City Boys championship. As he got better, the Atlanta Tennis Association helped him with travel expenses for attending out of town tournaments,

He became a formidable high school player, consistently winning his way to the finals of the Georgia Interscholastic Athletic Association's annual tennis shootout in Athens, Georgia, often meeting friend Sonny Mullis in the finals, who won the event many times. Allen won it for the first time in 1948; and was selected to play on the U.S. Junior Davis Cup team in '48 and '49.

Legendary Atlanta Boys High football coach Shorty Doyal, having been hired by Marist College[1] to build a football program, arranged for him to have a scholarship to the school, and he became the team's star quarterback. Tennis took a back seat. He set his goal on playing college football, made "All State", and was named Punter of the Year by the Georgia High School Athletic Association. In 1951, he received a grant-in-aid from Georgia Tech. Unfortunately his grades the first two quarters were not impressive and he decided to find another school.

Then the second life-changing event took place. Friend Sonny Mullis called, telling him Coach Jim Leighton at Presbyterian College was looking for tennis players and had scholarships available. He and Sonny hitchhiked to Clinton from Atlanta; both were offered a tennis scholarship. Sonny already had an offer from Young Harris college, and decided not to take the PC offer. Allen went, and worked with the team during the spring, being ineligible that year, and Coach Leighton told him if he kept his present style of play, he would be an acceptable college player, but began suggesting a radical change in his stroke production, which would require much hard work and commitment, and asked Allen to make the decision. He did, and worked tirelessly. The work paid off and his game took a quantum leap forward.

[1] *A private high school for boys, the name notwithstanding. It later became "the Marist School," co-ed.*

He worked out with the team daily from 1:30 in the afternoon to 5; at night they watched films of famous players, such as Don Budge's backhand.

During that first winter, Coach Leighton worked only on his backhand; later, they disassembled his forehand and put it back together again. The following summer, interested school supporters and Clinton residents created a fund to allow him to travel and play tournaments. His record was good enough to qualify him for the U. S. Championships, then played at Forest Hills, and his first round draw was Mervin Rose, a top ranked Australian Davis Cup player. Rose won, but was taken to five sets by the unknown college player from Clinton S.C. Playing for PC and Captain of the team, he was undefeated at No.1 singles in 1953 and 1954.

He won the South Carolina Intercollegiate Championship singles three years straight, and the doubles in '53 and '54. He was selected as an alternate member to the U.S. Davis Cup Team in '54, '55, and '56.

In the Wimbledon All-England Championships in 1956, Allen, then ranked No.16 in the U.S., took top ranked Vic Seixas to the wall in the quarterfinals, loosing in a match going a marathon 13-11 in the first set.

He won the Georgia State singles title in '57, the South Carolina singles in '57 and '58, the North Carolina singles in '58, '61, '63, '64, '65 and '67; and the doubles in '58, '62, '63, and '64. Other titles include the Eastern Clay Court singles, '59; New York state singles in '59 and '60 and doubles in '59 and '60; the Atlanta Invitational singles in'63; the North Carolina state singles 35's in '75 and '76; the Southern singles 35's in '76; the USTA National Clay singles 45's in '77 and '78 and the doubles in '77 and '78.

Wimbledon, 1956

After graduation from PC with a degree in Economics, he held various management positions in the textile industry for almost 25 years, continuing to be a top level tournament player, until 1980, when he became Head Tennis Coach and Director of Tennis at the University of North Carolina.

For the next 13 years, he complied a 245-123 record with five 20-win seasons and five ACC titles. He was named ACC Coach of the Year four times. He left UNC to return to his Alma Mater, Presbyterian College as the Director of Athletics. His success there led to his induction into the South Atlantic Conference Hall of Fame. Seven more followed; the N.C. Sports HOF, the N.C. Tennis HOF, the Southern Tennis HOF, the Intercollegiate Tennis HOF, the South Atlantic Conference HOF, the Guilford County Sports HOF, and the South Carolina Athletic HOF. He was three time Atlantic Coast Conference Men's Tennis Coach of the Year, '83, '90, and '92.; and the ITC Region II Wilson Coach of the Year in '92. PC won two Atlantic Coast Conference Championships, '91 and '92, under his leadership.

MANUEL DIAZ

MONSTER SERVER
MASTERFUL COACH

It happened on sudden death point, 4 all in a tie-breaker (the now seldom used Van Alen 5 pointer), Manuel playing No. 1 for Georgia against Pepperdine's Joavo Soares (later to star on Brazil's Davis Cup team) at UGA's Henry Feild Stadium on court No. I in 1975, before a large crowd, with the match even at a set apiece.

Soares chose to receive in the deuce court, and what he got was a huge topspin crosscourt delivery that bounced completely over his head, unreachable. It landed out of the court, over the small fence in the corner, in Magill's words *"plumb out of the arena."* The Club Pavilion seats weren't there then, but if they had been, the ball would have landed in someone's lap. The crowd went wild. But it didn't end there.

Manuel's racket had slipped out of his hand, and struck the net. Coach Riggs (the legendary Bobby Rigg's son) ran over to Coach Magill, and said the point belonged to Soares because Manuel's racket had hit the net. *"... I (Magill) told him I was not the umpire, and pointed to Dr. Blackstone in the chair.. . (who had Cherokee blood, and looked like an Indian chief) who replied, 'that's true; it did hit the net, but not until the ball had bounced over the fence and out of play, ending the point.' Riggs then turned to me and said, in resignation, "Well, all I got to say is, that's the damnedest serve I've ever seen..."*

"Well all I got to say is, that's the damnedest serve I've ever seen..."

Coach Riggs,
Pepperdine

COURTESY COLLEGIATE TENNIS HALL OF FAME

Playing for Georgia

"I'll never forget Manuel Diaz' first trip to the University of Georgia, in early April 1971, when we were playing a home match against Virginia.

"I was standing in the lobby of the Henry Feild clubhouse...when a tall handsome boy and his look- alike father introduced themselves. They were Manuel Diaz Sr., and Manolito, who had just arrived from Puerto Rico, without notice. They wanted to see where Manolito was considering spending his next four years. (I had offered Manuel Jr. a scholarship, sight unseen, on the recommendation of one of my former players, Tony Ortiz.

"A few days later, he mailed me his signed SEC grant-in-aid. He even then had the rudiments of a great topspin serve, taught him by Welby Van Horn, and was strong, fast, and a natural net rusher and volleyer who could jump unusually high to put away overheads. He had a beautiful slice backhand approach, but was little crude on his forehand drive and service return. He jumped from No. 6 to our No. 1 spot his sophomore year, after the graduation of All American Danny Birchmore, and won his first big tournament in February 1973, the Princeton Indoor....

"As a senior, he had one of the finest seasons ever by a Bulldog player. He won the SEC Championship... and in March 1975, upset NCAA Champion John Whitlinger before a huge crowd, serving 14 aces."

Dan Magill, 2009

Just as impressive as that epic serve is his coaching record, a near impossible 488-100 (.830) in 21 seasons. He was inducted into the Puerto Rico Hall of Fame in 1998, and the Georgia Tennis Hall of Fame in 2000.

In addition to his four NCAA Championships, his teams have reached the NCAA finals seven other times: 1989, 1991, 1993, 1997, 1998, 2002, and 2006. In addition, they have reached the semifinals twice and quarterfinals five times. Diaz has received many honors in collegiate tennis, including being selected as the Wilson/ITA National Coach-of-the Year in 1995, 2001 and 2007. Under Diaz, Georgia has been among the most nationally-televised of college tennis teams. UGA made history in 2007 when its national championship win in Athens at the Dan Magill Tennis Complex became the first collegiate tennis match to be televised live. The production was carried on ESPN.

He is married to the former Suzanne Rondeau of Toronto. They have three sons, Manuel III, Eric, and Alex.

COURTESY GEORGIA TENNIS HALL OF FAME

KENNY THORN
HEAD COACH, MENS TENNIS
GEORGIA TECH

GEORGIA TECH SPORTS INFORMATION DEPARTMENT

We all have Walter Mitty dreams. And if one could be bought, many would line up to buy Kenny's. He's one of those few who successfully climb a very slippery slope: college tennis at an academically tough school, followed by success on the pro tennis tour for eight years; followed by a stellar coaching career; and coupled with a successful marriage and four children.

He played on the ATP tour for eight years, winning seven titles, with wins over four of the world's top-10 players in the 1990's, the best being over 1996 Wimbledon champion Richard Peter Stanislav Krajicek, five years his junior; ATP No. 11 Wayne Ferreira; Australia's Mark Philippoussis; and Todd Martin of the United States. His highest singles ranking was 121, doubles 67. He was a six-time participant at Wimbledon, and competed yearly at the U.S., French, and Australian Opens while on tour. His best career wins were He posted two career ATP doubles titles, one Challenger singles title and four Challenger doubles titles.

Who would have ever dreamed that an American kid playing junior tournaments in the 70's would, just a few years later, be making money winning a tournament in Asia (Seoul, Korea) with a French partner (Stephane Simian), and just a few months later win another one in Italy with an Australian partner.

An All-American in 1988, Thorne finished his Georgia Tech playing career as a four-time All-ACC honoree and the career leader in singles victories with 112. He was also a two-time captain and an Academic All-ACC honoree.

During his four seasons as a player from 1985-1988, the Jackets posted a 70-38 dual-match record and a 20-7 ACC mark, including wins over nationally ranked foes such as Georgia and Clemson in 1988, his final season.

He was inducted into the Ga. Tech Athletic Hall of Fame in 1995; named Director of Tennis and Head Coach of the men's team in 1998, and inducted into the Georgia Tennis Hall of Fame in 2006.

In 1999 he became the first person in ACC history, and the second nationally, to lead the same school as a player, assistant coach and head coach since the current NCAA team dual-match format was instituted in 1977. Thorne helped Tech in NCAA play as a senior in 1988, as an assistant coach in 1998 and as head coach in 1999.

In his first year as head coach, he earned ACC Coach of the Year honors after guiding his team to a second-place tie in the regular season conference standings, a runner-up finish at the ACC Tournament, an NCAA Regional berth and a final national ranking of 32 by the Intercollegiate Tennis Association.

SIDE BY SIDE. Ga. Tech's two coaches have striking similarities and followed almost parallel paths to where they both are today. Both were outstanding junior players coached by the legendary Bill Tym, meeting each other many times in tournaments, both electing not to just go to college, but

BRIAN SHELTON
HEAD COACH, WOMENS' TENNIS
GEORGIA TECH

He was an oddity among his fellow ATP players in the 1990's, a player who actually graduated from college.

At Tech, he earned All-American honors and All-Atlantic Coast Conference as a player, and, oh yes, the dean's list for four years straight. His education at the prestigious Randolph School, a private prep school in Huntsville, AL, (the "Rocket City") where he grew up, no doubt gave him an academic leg up. Virtually all Randolph grads go on to attain four year college degrees. Randolph has always had a strong tennis program, and was one of the first schools to require all 8th-12th grade students to have wireless-capable laptops. Before turning pro, he won the United States Amateur Championship in 1985 (the tournament was begun in 1968, the year marking the beginning of "open tennis," as a tournament for those wishing to compete with other amateurs.)

After graduation, he entered the pro tour, where most never come close to making expenses. In Shelton's first year, he broke through the world top 100 and surpassed $1MM in ATP prize money. He was the first African-American to win an ATP title since Arthur Ashe, who was his role model.

He played Wimbledon six times, and would eventually win four ATP titles, and a career ranking of 55 in singles and 52 in doubles. Two of the singles wins, 1991 and 1992, were on grass, at the historic Newport Casino.

GEORGIA TECH SPORTS INFORMATION

One of his long suits was his kick serve. He delivered 40 aces in a 4 setter in the Australian Open in 1991, the first year they started counting. That record held for the next 6 years.

He upset #2 seed Michael Stich in the 1994 Wimbledon to reach the round of 16, along the way taking out ATP giants Andre Agassi, Richard Krajicek, Todd Martin and Tomas Muster.

He reached the mixed doubles final of the French Open in 1994, with partner Lori McNeil. He was elected to the ATP Tour Player's Council in 1995.

He coached Malivai Washington, 1996 Wimbledon finalist, for a time, and worked a stint as a USTA national coach. In 1999 he returned to his alma mater as coach of the Women's' team, bringing them to a school best of No. 29.

Another oddity, he's a superb athlete who's modest. He claims his sister Yudda, an All-American in track and field at the University of Alabama, was the best one in the family, .

His coaching record at Tech includes a 2007 NCAA Div. I National Championship, the first ever for Georgia Tech. Other coaching accomplishments include the 2007 and 2008 ITA National Indoor Team Championships and the 2005, 2006, and 2007 ACC Championships.

He and his wife live in Atlanta with their two children.

---

choosing an academically challenging major, Industrial Engineering at Ga. Tech. Both earned academic honors there while achieving stellar playing records and went on to successful ATP careers, retiring at almost the same time. The Ga. Tech Alumni magazine dubbed them "A Perfect Match."

WALTER JOHNSON

Kids are taught not to throw their rackets. Apparently no one told Wally not to.[1]

This remarkable photo demonstrates "never give up" in the extreme. Johnson eventually lost in three sets, but reached the semis with partner Paul Speicher. He came to Tech with credentials. Growing up in Hollywood Florida, the son of tournament playing City Champions Walter Sr. and Susan, he was one of the top juniors nationally in all junior age groups, and a member of the U.S. Junior Davis Cup team. He played in the Orange Bowl, International Tennis Federation's elite event for boys 16 and under, following in the footsteps of such world class players as Marcos Baghdatis, Andy Roddick, Roger Federrer, and Ivan Lendl.

He was recruited by Georgia Tech coach Jack Rogers (the first head pro at Bitsy Grant Tennis Center in the early '50's). While a student, he won the Atlanta City and Georgia State Opens. His singles record percentage of .818 at Tech is second only to Harry Thompson's. He reached a national singles ranking of 25 in 1967. His style of play, physically overpowering with a blistering flat serve and an intimidating swinging volley was unique in the era of wooden rackets. Had it not been for several knee operations, he might have become a contender on the pro circuit at the ideal time, the initial years of "open tennis" after 1968. Instead he took the head pro position with John Newcombe's T Bar M Tennis Ranch in Texas' hill country of New Braunfels. Back in Atlanta in 1972, he began his along association with the Capital City Club, and again won the Atlanta City Open, in 1973. He was Georgia Tech's third All-American player, and in 1974, became Tech's tennis coach for the next nine years.

ASSOCIATED PRESS, BY PERMISSION

Walter Johnson, 1966 NCAA Division I finals, Miami FL

[1] *By today's rules, if the player is not holding the racket when it strikes the ball, he looses the point.*

MIKAEL PERNFORS

Born in Malmo Sweden in 1963, he came to the U.S. on his own, without a scholarship, to play tennis and go to college[1]. He won back-to-back NCAA singles titles in 1984 and 1985. The record The overflow gallery of 4500 at the 1984 event was the largest ever (at that time) to have watched a collegiate tennis match.

He became a regular on the ATP Tour, in spite of being plagued with injuries most of his career. His most significant win was the Canadian Open in 1993. His ATP career high world ranking was No. 10, in 1986.

He defeated many top players, including Andre Agassi in 1988, and had an infamous win over John McEnroe in the Australian Open in 1990, when McEnroe became the first player to be disqualified under a new Code of Conduct that three code violations would result in disqualification (instead of the previous four). Pernfors won the match by default after McEnroe attempted to intimidate a lineswoman, smashed a racket, and then verbally abused the umpire.

He continues to play senior events. A laid-back, mild mannered guy, he takes things in stride, and has his priorities straight. His career earnings were just over $1,000,000, far below what some earn in a single year now, but he's a happy guy.

Some insight into his personality is revealed in an interview between matches at an exhibition event recently in the Cayman Islands: What do you like most about playing on the Legends tour? *"The camaraderie with all the players I used to play with."* What do you think about the possibility of playing Pete Sampras on another Legends tour event? *"I don't want to think about that..."* Did you get out to the Sting Ray City or do any other things while in Cayman? *"I came with my wife and 3-1/2-year-old, so we mainly stayed by the pool."* You seem to have a lot of fun when you're playing. Is that intentional? *"We're not as good as we used to be. I think the people understand that."*

After winning the
1984 NCAA finals

"Our greatest player was a little Swede named Michael Pernfors. I almost didn't give him a scholarship. He was small, just over 5' 7", but his coach down there at the junior college in Sanford said he was good...

"I wasn't going to give him a scholarship, but... I got a letter from Boris Becker, who I was trying to recruit, saying 'Dear Herr Magill, thank you for the scholarship offer, but I've just been selected to the German Davis Cup team and I won't....(be accepting your offer)...'

"Then Paul Groth called me up and he said, "I understand you're interested in this little Swede, Michael Pernfors." I said, 'Yeah, have you ever seen him play?' He said, 'yeah, he just beat me in the finals of a professional tournament down here. I played as a pro, he played as an amateur... You better give him a scholarship. He'll be the best damn player you ever had...'

"In his first workout, my assistant coach Manuel Diaz, said Pernfors could hit the ball off balance better than anybody he had ever seen. He was just very agile - very strong from the waist up..."

Dan Magill, 2009

---

[1] Seminole State, part of the Florida College System, is located in Sanford, FL and not renowned for its athletic programs. Pernfors is one of its most distinguished alumni.

COURTESY COLLEGIATE TENNIS HALL OF FAME

Allen Miller, above on the right, with partner Ola Malmqvist winning the 1983 NCAA doubles in Athens, Georgia

ALLEN MILLER

Allen Miller, as a young boy in Tucker, learned to play tennis at the nearby DeKalb Tennis Center in Decatur. His coach there was former Tulane star Crawford Henry, NCAA doubles champion in 1957 and 1959.

Miller earned All-America honors four years (1982-85), the first University of Georgia athlete to do so in any sport. As a freshman he and his tall (6' 7") teammate Ola Malmqvist won the ITA National Indoor doubles and were finalists in the NCAA doubles; and the next year they won it.

As a senior in 1985 Miller scored important points in both singles and doubles as Georgia defeated UCLA in the Team Tournament finals. He holds the NCAA Tournament record for best career mark in doubles since the NCAA Team Tournament began in 1977. Counting Team Tournament and individual tournament doubles matches, Miller owns a 22-4 record; he also set the modern day mark of best-average finish in NCAA doubles: finals in '82, winner in '83, and semi-finalist in both '84 and '85. He and Mikael Pernfors finished the '85 season as the nation's No. 1 ranked doubles team.

Miller is now director of tennis at Athens (Georgia) Country Club.

"I started playing at Dekalb; Crawford Henry was my first coach. He left Dekalb when I was about 14, and my family joined WCT (World Championship Tennis) and I started working with Gary Groslimond there, and some with Ricky Bodin.

"I went to Kalamazoo starting in the 12's; my best record was in the 18's, when I got to the semis in the consolation.

"I played some satellite events (sponsored then by the ATP, before the International Tennis Federation Futures and Challengers circuit). I stuck with it for about six months, and during that time I might have collected a few hundred dollars, maybe $400 once when I got to the finals of one of them. My expenses probably ran about $15,000 during that period. My father had passed away, and I had family obligations, and on top of that I had met my future (and now present) wife, so I decided to hang it up and go back to school and finish. I'm happy where I am now, I made the right decision. "

Allen Miller, 2010

"The first time I saw Joseph Allen Miller Jr. make some of his uncanny shots was in the Crackerland Boys' 10's singles final in Athens in the summer of 1973. He lost to David Wilder of Macon, son of Mercer basketball coach Bobby Wilder, but I remember remarking to Dr. Robert H. West, then President of the Athens Tennis Association, that the skinny lefthander was a gifted shotmaker and would be heard from some day. He won the Crackerland Boys' 18 singles in 1981, and Georgia was just one of many schools trying to recruit him. Luckily we got him. In my opinion he could still be playing professional tennis as a doubles player. He was the best college doubles player I've ever seen. "

Dan Magill, "Oral History of the University of Georgia"

LISA SPAIN SHORT

Lisa's plaque in the Georgia Tennis Hall of Fame states that her coach, when she began playing, at age 7, Mike Jenkins of the Moultrie Recreation Department, was at the time teaching himself to play.

By reading a book.

He was charging the family $1/hour. And he remained her coach for the next eleven years, and became, in her words, *"part of the family,"* working with her countless hours, each becoming more proficient in their respective half of the partnership.

Learning the game by reading a book is reminiscent of another, considerably older, player, the legendary Carrie Howell, matriarch of one of Georgia's first families of tennis, who claimed she did the same, learned from reading a how-to book, without a coach.

The odds against most beginners becoming a four time Georgia State high school champion and an NCAA Women's singles winner are staggering even for those with the best available coaching that money can buy, which is most often found only in large cities. Add to that playing on the WTA and the odds shoot off the chart. But Lisa is clearly not like "most."

She would daily ride her bicycle, or sometimes her Shetland pony, to the courts, and stay until dark. If Mike was not available, she worked with her "other coach", a backboard. The formula worked, and by her last year in high school she was in the top three in the state, and the top twenty in the Southern Region. She racked up an almost unbelievable 56-1 record during high school competition. She was the first woman player in the University of Georgia's history to be awarded a scholarship, and led the school's move to becoming a national tennis powerhouse, gaining All-American honors in 1981.

COURTESY GEORGIA TENNIS HALL OF FAME

She surprised a few people when she upset a higher ranked Stanford player, Linda Gates, in 1984, to win the NCAA singles, following the footsteps of Wendy White-Prausa, the only other Georgia winner of the event at that time, who won in 1970.

She won the ITCA All American singles in the fall of 1984. After graduating, she played on the WTA circuit until 1987, sponsored by avid tennis fan and University of Georgia benefactor (who funded construction of the Collegiate Tennis Hall of Fame) Kenny Rogers, the country music star (married at the time to Athens Georgia native Marianne).

She broke through the top 75, reaching a career high of 63, and reached the finals of the French in 1981.

She played all four grand slam events for four straight years, competing against Navratilova, Evert, Graf, and others at the pinnacle of the sport. She played Wimbledon four times, '83 - '86, and in '85 she had a match point against Graf. Her best Wimbledon win was in 1986, defeating Sylvia Hanika, no. 5 in the world at the time. Some tennis fans may remember Hanika's distracting eccentricity, of bouncing the ball repeatedly when preparing to serve. Bud Collins frequently remarked on it, and likened her multiple bounces to hearing a faucet drip, seeming to never end; and on the agony of another 30 or so bounces if she missed the first serve. Apparently Lisa's concentration was not shaken by it. Had she continued with WTA play, she well might have broken through the top 5 or better. She was inducted into the Southern Tennis Hall of Fame in 2008.

Lisa enjoyed a dream career; a spectacular high school record, a meteoric assent into the thin air of college tennis' top levels, and a four year run with the best in the world. Then, having shown all that she could tame the beast, blithely withdrawing to go in another direction. She put it all aside for marriage to a college sweetheart and three children. Perhaps she planned it that way all along. According to Coach Magill, "*...she wanted to*

HARRY THOMPSON

His day job is CEO of Conklin Metal, a four generation family business whose history goes back to 1874, still going strong. A list of successful businesses that old anywhere in the world would be a short one; not even the Coca Cola Company would qualify.

One of the top junior players in the South in the mid-1950's, he started playing at age 12 at the Piedmont Driving Club, coached by pro Jack Waters.

One year after starting, he won both the singles and doubles in Dan Magill's Crackerland tournament in the 15 and under age division. Two years later he was ranked No. 1 in the South in the 15's singles, and No. 2 in doubles with partner Ned Neely. His development was no accident. Waters personally took many of his protégés' to important junior tournaments, such as Davidson, N. C. for the Southern Championships, Champagne, IL for the Western Championships, and Kalamazoo, MI for the National Championships for juniors.

He entered Westminster Schools in 1951 in the 8th grade, the year the school was started, continuing to be coached there by Waters. The school dominated high school tennis in Georgia for decades, and in 1956 won the National Interscholastic title, Thompson reaching the doubles finals with partner Neely.

Entering Georgia Tech in 1958 on a tennis scholarship, he won the No. 3 singles in the SEC finals that year. He holds the individual player career winning record at Georgia Tech. In 1959, the team that year finished 19-2, a record that still stands. In 1960, he and partner Dave Peake won the Georgia Interscholastic doubles in Athens, Ga.

After a stint in the U.S. Navy, he resumed tournament play, always ranked highly in both singles and doubles, for many years No. 1 in the south in doubles, with partners John Skogstad (All American, U. of Miami), Bob Nichols, Ned Neely, John Foster, and Lindsey Hopkins. He has served the Atlanta Lawn Tennis Association in various capacities continuously for many years, as President in 1967-1970. He was inducted into the Georgia Tennis Hall of Fame in 1970.

1952 Atlanta City Junior Singles winner

JOHN SKOGSTAD

In 1956, playing in Florida's Orange Bowl tournament, he took out Ron Holmberg, who later that year defeated Rod Laver in the Junior Wimbledon. John had lost earlier that year to Laver in the fourth round of Kalamazoo in the 18's.

In Kalamazoo he met several Atlanta players, and their coach, Jack Waters, including Harry Thompson, who would later take over his family's business in Atlanta, Conklin Metal. John was employed by Conklin Metal, now retired.

While in high school in Coral Gables, FL, where he grew up, he won the National Interscholastic Championships doubles with Bobby Macy, representing Coral Gables High. After a year at Baylor, he switched to the University of Miami, which had a record breaking year, and he was named All-American, joining an elite group of alumni from that institution, including greats Garner Mulloy, Vic Seixas, and three time NCAA singles champion Pancho Segura.

In 1961 in the Atlanta Invitational, at age 28, he was up a set and a break against a college player, Arthur Ashe, much younger, who had just won the NCAA singles title. Ashe was the tournament's main gate attraction. Hmmm. Ashe remained in the tournament, went on to victory, and the fans were not disappointed.

A year later, he extended Frank Froeling, (U. S. Championships runner-up, 1963, No. 6 in the world at the time and three years younger than John) to three sets. He was playing "the circuit", such as it was at that time, before open tennis, against full time players such as Laver, Rosewall, Stolle, and Emerson. John could only play a few tournaments when his work schedule would allow him to take a few days off.

He has always been highly ranked in his age group, mostly at No. 1. He has seven national titles, playing with Atlanta partners Walt Massey, Jerry Caldwell, and Joe Becknell.

COURTESY HARRY THOMPSON

He's a member of the Southern and the Georgia Tennis Halls of Fame. He's served the Atlanta tennis community in many ways, for several years as president of the Atlanta Lawn Tennis Association in the 70's, and Vice President of the Georgia Tennis Association. In the '60's, he was always associated as one of the "big three" in Atlanta; himself, Crawford Henry, and Ned Neely.

REBECCA BIRCHMORE CAMPEN

Becky is a rarity; an attractive girl with superior intellect and exceptional athletic talent. Women have long been regarded in many cultures as athletic inferiors. Perhaps on average they are, but then Becky is not average.

When she attended the University of Georgia as an undergraduate, Title IX legislation was years in the future, and there were no women's athletic teams in the SEC. She had won the Georgia State Open Women's singles twice. Then in 1963, the SEC ruled that women could play sports on men's teams.

Becky tried out for and made the men's' tennis team that year, as a senior. She won all her matches, and was the first, the last, and the only woman ever to earn a men's tennis varsity letter at the University of Georgia.

A lot of men expressed more than just reservation about the SEC ruling. It was more akin to terror. There was talk of female linebackers. During Becky's senior year at UGA, Martha Leveritt swam on the Emory men's team against Tulane, and Roberta Allison made the men's tennis team at Alabama, causing attendance to soar when she played. She and the team were undefeated through their first five matches in 1963.

A few years later, there would be a promotional smattering of men playing against women, one of the first being the famed "Battle of the Sexes" Billie Jean King/Bobby Riggs match up (which left a humbled but richer Riggs to lick his wounds and eat some of his pre-match words).

Tennis is not her only achievement. After earning her bachelor's degree, she went on to get a masters in medical microbiology, then a law degree, then an MD. She maintains a law practice, and is director of the Cutaneous Biology Research Center at Harvard.

COURTESY COLLEGIATE TENNIS HALL OF FAME

Above, Becky Birchmore receives the ITA Rolex Lifetime Achievement Award, flanked by, L to R, U. S. Senator John Breaux, Roland Putan, CEO Rolex USA, and tennis legend Stan Smith at the 1995 U.S. Open in New York. She later received UGA's Bill Hartman Award, the highest honor a former UGA student athlete can attain.

She comes from a family of over achievers, all of whom have advanced degrees in various fields. Her father, Freddie Birchmore, an Athens, Georgia icon, earned his law degree from UGA and was the SEC bantamweight boxing champion in 1930. In 1935, 25 year old Freddie circled the globe via bicycle, which he named Bucephalus[1], a journey of some 25,000 miles. The journey involved partially retracing the steps of Marco Polo, through wild countries, including Afghanistan. Bucephalus is now on display in the Smithsonian museum in Washington DC.

More recently father Freddie captured the attention of all of Athens Georgia when he decided, at age 75, to erect a high stone wall, 18' in places, around his two acre home site, "Happy Hollow," single handedly, using 12 train boxcar loads of large stones, taking over five years.

In addition to law and real estate, he's been a college professor, a singer, scout leader, a collector of Indian relics, a lecturer on Indian folklore, a respected ornithologist, a free lance writer, an aviator, a Naval gunnery officer in WWII, and a champion tennis player and coach.

Fred on Bucephalus ca 1935

---

[1] *Named for Alexander the Great's horse, "Bucephalus"*

ARTHUR (SPEED) HOWELL

One of his early contacts with tennis was helping Harry Thompson run the coke stand at Bitsy Grant Tennis Center during a tournament shortly after the center opened in 1952. Ironically, his first win was, reputedly, beating the coke stand boy in the first round of the consolation of his first tournament, the Southern Juniors at Davidson College, when he was 12, having lost a first round match. For this first tournament he and other junior players piled into Jack Waters' station wagon for the drive up. He spent the week playing and watching others, among them Ned Neely and Harry Thompson, play their matches and listening to Coach Waters' critique.

Mother Carrie had earlier informed him, under protest, that he would soon start taking lessons from Jack Waters, even though "...*its not even summer yet!*" At some point the protests must have stopped, because he spent every summer day thereafter playing, and going with Waters to various tournaments, many far away, such as the Westerns, and the National Juniors at Kalamazoo, where, in his first year there, he saw Rod Layer win the 18's, and Ned Neely win the 15's.

His most notable win in Kalamazoo was over Arthur Ashe, in doubles. He later won the Mid-South doubles with three different partners, Mike Neely, Charlie Benedict, and Carleton Fuller, while winning his singles division each year. He won the Georgia State High School Championship as a senior.

See also p. 114

RICHARD HOWELL

1966, on his way to a fourth straight GIAA title

He was an early starter (age 6) and an early bloomer (finals of the Georgia State 13's doubles at age 7). So avidly did he pursue all other sports, however, including football, basketball, and baseball, that he rarely played tennis in the fall and winter, until he reached college.

He played some spectacular junior matches; in the Georgia State 11 and under at Bitsy, he blitzed a young Stanley Pasarell, considered at the time the No. 1 age 11 and under player in the world, incredibly losing only a single point in the first set. He won two Southern Open Junior Singles Championships at Davidson, NC, and the doubles five times. A tennis star for Westminster Schools in Atlanta, he won the AAA Georgia State High School singles championship four consecutive times, and was a runner-up in the tough Atlanta City Mens Open (while still in high school) and in the Georgia State Open Mens doubles at age 15. He was consistently ranked in the top 5 nationally in both singles and doubles.

He won the USTA National Boys 14's doubles with partner Zan Guerry in 1962, and they finished the year with a No. 1 ranking. He quit junior tournaments at age 17 and started playing Open events to prepare for college. He was offered a tennis scholarship from a dozen schools, including Georgia. Tech and the University of Georgia. He chose Princeton (in the family tradition). He played at various times No. 1, 2, or 3, and was within a hair of an undefeated collegiate tennis career, with only one loss. He played tournaments after graduation, and was consistently ranked in the top 3 in Georgia in singles, and with partner Bill Shippey, had an incredible run of 7 years without losing a match.

See also p. 114

PETER HOWELL

A graduate of Vanderbilt University, he starred for three seasons for the Commodores before injury sidelined him his senior year. As a junior he was named captain of the team and Most Valuable Player.

> *"If you don't, I'll tell mother..."*

Peter comes from a family steeped in tennis tradition. In 1964, the Howell family was selected as the Tennis Family-of-the-Year by the Southern Tennis Association. Peter was inducted as a member of the Georgia Tennis Hall of Fame in 2010, joining brother Richard and mother Carrie. He's the only one of the Howells to choose tennis as a career.

COURTESY BARBARA HOWELL

A doubles specialist, he and partner Woody Hoblitzell have been ranked nationally many times; No.9 in 35's doubles in '87 and No. 5 in '88 and '89; and No. 5 in 40's doubles in '90, '91, and '92. He's held a Georgia ranking of No.1 in almost every age group.

He's won (not surprisingly) many tournaments, including the Atlanta City Open Doubles, the Georgia State Open and State Closed Doubles, the Open Indoor Doubles, the Georgia State Indoor Mixed Doubles, the Atlanta City Open Mixed Doubles, the Georgia State Open Mixed Doubles and the 35's and the 40's doubles many times.

> *When I was 9, Jack Waters, the pro at the Driving Club, thought my much older brother Richard (age 10) and I should play together in a tournament. When we started, Richard scratched an X in the alley, and said "...Peter, stay right here..." To make sure I understood, he added, "...if you don't, I'll tell Mother..."*
>
> *Peter Howell*

He began playing at age 9 at the Piedmont Driving Club, and went undefeated his senior year at Episcopal High School in Virginia. He started his professional teaching career in 1971 at the Atlanta Athletic Club, later joining Ansley Golf Club in 1979. In 1983 he began a pilot program with the City of Atlanta, leasing the Bitsy Grant facility, where he remained until 1988. He was head pro at the Standard Club in Atlanta from 1988 to 2000. He is currently coach of Oglethorpe University's tennis team, now ranked No. 7 in the Atlantic South Division of NCAA D-3. At Oglethorpe he operates the Peter Howell Tennis Camp for junior players in June and July each year.

He's been an active volunteer in many organizations. He founded, in 1977, the Georgia Professional Tennis Association, now with over 300 members. In the Georgia Tennis Association he's chaired almost every committee and served as its executive vice-president. In the Southern Tennis Association he's served as Sanction & Scheduling Chairman. Long active in the Bitsy Grant Tennis Association, he spearheaded the effort to renovate the historic public facility, for years in a steady decline, raising millions of dollars and resulting in a total makeover of the building and the courts in 2011.

92

JACK RODGERS

JACK RODGERS

He was the first head tennis professional at Bitsy Grant Tennis Center when it opened in 1952. He coached the Georgia Tech Men's tennis team for many years.

HOWARD MCCALL

HOWARD MCCALL

Howard McCall was a three year letterman at Georgia Tech under Coach Earl Bortell, and a perennial doubles partner of Frank Willett.

HORACE REID

HORACE REID

He turned out not just good, but very good. Under Branch Currington's tutelage, he progressed rapidly, and won the National Boys 16's doubles in 1971 with partner Billy Martin, in Kalamazoo, rocketing him into the lofty thin air of the likes of later winners John McEnroe, Al Parker, and more recently the Bryan brothers. His state championship wins in 1970 and 1971, while attending Booker T. Washington High, were no surprise. He earned a tennis scholarship to UCLA and played there from 1973 until 1975. After college he played on the ATP tour for two years, earning a world ranking of #269. A few years later, he won the USTA National Clay Singles 35's, and in 2001, won the Atlanta Senior Invitational 45's at Bitsy Grant Tennis Center. He's now a teaching professional in Atlanta. He was inducted into the Georgia Tennis Hall of Fame in 1997.

> "...several of us were playing...(at Washington Park)...when a little boy hung over the fence..."..."what do you want, boy?... 'just lookin' he said (to pro Branch Currington)..."what's your name?" 'Horace Reid...'... "you want to play this game?"... 'Yes sir'... "...then I'm going to give you a racket, and I want you here every morning at ten o'clock..."
>
> 'Making My Mark' - - Marvin Arrington.

JEFF WALLACE

Courtesy Georgia Tennis Hall of Fame

"I got started in tennis by accident when I was 12. A friend and I were at a summer camp in Oregon. We were riding horses, and my friend got thrown and didn't want to ride any more, so we found an old beat up tennis court at the camp, and that's all we did for the rest of the time. I had found a new sport..."
Jeff Wallace, 2009

He did pretty well with the new sport, ranked No. 2 in the Oregon 18's, and eventually won a tennis scholarship to Utah State, where he played for two years. By chance, the NCAA championships were held in Athens, Georgia both years, and when he saw the wild enthusiasm for tennis at UGA, he decided to transfer, and played his junior and senior years for UGA at No. 6 singles. After graduation he became a student assistant coach in 1985 when UGA won their first NCAA Championship. He became coach of the UGA Womens' tennis team in 1986 and turned a loosing prior season record around, going 20-9, and the following year coached the team to the NCAA finals. He was named Coach of the Year. His teams have finished in the top 10 in 21 of his 24 years coaching; and 40% of his players have been named All-American.

Jeff Wallace

DANIEL ALEXANDER BIRCHMORE

Courtesy Collegiate Tennis Hall of Fame

The youngest Birchmore son, Danny, an All-American tennis player at Georgia where he was captain of the championship Bulldogs, won the USTA National Boy's 18's singles in 1969 in Kalamazoo. In 1971 he lead Georgia to its first SEC team title in tennis, winning at No. 1 singles. He earned All-American honors in 1971-72, and the 1971 Rafael Osuna Award, collegiate tennis' highest honor, voted on by the players and given to the player best demonstrating good sportsmanship and competitive excellence. He was inducted into the Georgia Tennis Hall of Fame in May, 2011.

"Fred (Birchmore's father) obviously expected great things from Danny. He named him for a biblical hero and for the immortal warrior Alexander the Great. He was not a natural shotmaker; he had an unusual style of blocking the ball instead of really stroking it; but he had uncanny timing, and could hit the ball on the rise most of the time. He was smart; he skipped a grade, and entered college at 17, and as a freshman he played No. 1 for us. He had a good year, going 14-4 in dual matches. He won the National Boys' 18's Clay the following summer, the only entrant who had played college tennis, and in the process upset Jimmy Connors in the quarters and Harold Solomon in the finals. He was a big drawing card for us, and often over 2000 came out when he played. There were near 3000 watching in April 1972 when we played Miami, who ended our 76 match winning streak, watching Danny loose a close three setter to future top 10 player Eddie Dibbs. His remarkable academic achievements won him a post-graduate scholarship. He passed up a professional playing career, and studied medicine."

Dan Magill

GORDON SMITH,
EXECUTIVE DIRECTOR AND
CHIEF OPERATING OFFICER, USTA

Georgia tennis players have a friend in court at the highest level. Years ago, as a partner in the King and Spalding law firm in Atlanta, he became general counsel for the Southern Tennis Association, and things went from there.

In 2007 he became the head of the United States Tennis Association. Many may think of USTA as just the outfit you mail your check to in order to play on a league team, but it's actually the world's largest tennis organization, and there's a lot going on behind the scenes. It owns and operates the U S Open, the largest sporting event in the world, and its 10 linked summer tournaments. In addition, it owns the 94 Pro Circuit events throughout the U.S., and selects the teams for the Davis Cup, Federation Cup, and the Olympic and Paralympic Games. It's a not-for-profit operation that plows 100% of its revenues back into the sport, with 700,000 members.

He was a star on four University of Georgia SEC championship teams, '72, '73, '74, and '75. His roommate (and doubles partner) in McWhorter Hall was none other than Manuel Diaz, now coach of the UGA men's' team. In addition to the SEC titles, they won the Southern Collegiate Championship, the Princeton Indoor, and went to the quarters of the 1975 NCAA doubles, having to default because of Manny's hospitalizing heat prostration.

Playing for UGA

He grew up in Rome, Georgia, and while attending Darlington School, he won the Georgia High School Singles Championship.

Many attorneys active in litigation know him from his days in the courtroom as a high profile defense lawyer. At King & Spalding, he was a senior litigation partner, concentrating on the defense of large product liability suits and other front page tort cases. He has served as lead trial and appellate counsel for a number of the country's largest tobacco, automotive, pharmaceutical and heavy equipment manufacturers. He is a fellow of the American College of Trial Lawyers and past chair of the American Bar Association Committee on Product Liability litigation.

He's a proponent of some novel ideas. In a speech recently to the Greater Rome Georgia Chamber of Commerce, he threw out a proposal that turned more than a few heads; construction of a 74 court tennis center in Rome, Ga, which would make it the largest tennis center in the country. He has done his homework, and cited reasons why such a facility near Mount Berry Square mall would make perfect sense for Rome, Floyd County and the whole state of Georgia.

A study conducted by the University of Georgia indicates that at the low end, the facility would bring $15 million in direct economic benefits to the Rome area. A single event, the 2009 Southern Sectionals in Mobile AL, with its large facility, earned an estimated $5 million. Rome, already a well known tennis community in the center of the USTA's Southern Region, could expect the same. Secondly, tennis nationally is growing at a phenomenal rate; more than 30 million players in 2009, an increase of 7 million in one year. Major tennis events require a large number of courts. If he's right, we might see mega-center tennis facilities catching on all over. If a single event can bring in $5 million, 74 courts could be paid off in a hurry.

See also p. 137

CHARLIE COX

Very few of us can look back knowing that we changed the course of history.

He can, and he did.

In 1970 two things happened that caused tennis to explode in Atlanta, and later in the whole country, and ultimately make a lot of money for a lot of people, mostly teaching pros and companies selling tennis clothing and equipment.

First, Charlie Cox, a Delta airline pilot, was elected president of ALTA;[1] and second, Atlanta was passed over as the site for a major national tournament that the ALTA board wanted, due to a perceived lack of manpower and funding to handle the event.

ALTA at that time was a small group of 10-12 individuals who worked tirelessly to stage tournaments. Disappointed by the loss of that tournament, Cox began to consider ways to attract members and generate money. Ruth Lay, a teaching pro in Atlanta at the time, had successfully staged interclub matches in Atlanta between various private clubs. Several ideas were considered, but the "home run" was to turn tennis into a team sport, teams competing in a league during a season of a fewmonths, and an end of season playoff between the leaders. His idea was to arrange players by skill level, calling seasoned tournament players "A," good club players "B," and novices "C."

To test the interest of potential league players, he set up a meeting to present his idea, and rented a room at the Squire Inn on Piedmont Road the evening of January 24, 1971.

COURTESY CHARLIE COX

To insure good participation, a film was to be shown, "*Great Moments in Tennis History,*" featuring Don Budge, Bill Tilden, Rod Laver, and other famous players. The objective was to recruit members, who would pay a "donation" of $5 for adults, and $1 for junior players. 246 people showed up, trying to squeeze into a room set up with 50 chairs. The film was shown, but it was anticlimactic.

Two months later, 90 teams had been formed, with over 900 players. Charlie described it as like breaking a rock with a hammer and finding solid gold inside. Today, ALTA, with 80,000 players, is the largest league in the world. It has divisions for men, women, juniors, seniors, wheelchair players, Sunday women, Thursday women, and on and on and on.

Charlie learned to play at the Piedmont Driving Club in Atlanta under Jack Waters' tutelage. A tall (6' 5") natural athlete, he made the freshman tennis and basketball teams at Georgia Tech in 1949 but interrupted his college to fly 20 combat missions for the Air Force during the Korean conflict. He returned to Tech for one season of varsity tennis in 1956. He then began to play seriously, and has been ranked No. 1 in Georgia in every age division from the 35's through the 70's, twice making No. 1 in the Southern rankings.

---

[1] An acronym, still officially the Atlanta Lawn Tennis Association, one of the few tennis organizations to retain the word "lawn" in their name.

Tennis is a family affair, including wife Ann, daughters Becky (Furman tennis scholarship) and Catherine (ranked No.1 in her age group numerous times) and son Bud (Auburn tennis scholarship). Bud has made a life out of tennis, and is now a teaching pro in Atlanta, after 5 successful years on the ATP, playing 5 Wimbledon's and several U.S. and French Opens.

Once during a pro tournament in Atlanta, legend Rod Laver was looking for a hitting partner, and Bud was recruited for the job. Laver commented later that he was glad he would not have to face Bud in the tournament. Bud got better and better, and Charlie recalled recently that one of the biggest thrills of his life was watching Bud play in that first Wimbledon.

COURTESY CHARLIE COX

6'6" Bud Cox towers over his hitting partner, tennis legend Rod Laver, 5'7"

COURTESY CHARLIE COX

Charlie, with a Wilson T-2000 racket, ca 1970.

Jimmy Connors made the T-2000 famous but many amateurs found it's 70 square inch head too difficult to manage. A solid hit had lots of zip, but off-center hits could be disastrous. For smooth stroking Charlie, no problem.

Together Bud and Charlie have played numerous father-son events. They won both the national USTA Super Senior father-son hard court and indoor (two events, two separate places) in 2000, placed third in the clay that year, then won the indoor and clay in 2001. They had reached the finals of the grass in 1995, were third in the clay in 1996 and 1997, and in the finals of the indoor in 2002.

The family's contributions to tennis are numerous; the Georgia Tennis Association recognized them at the "Tennis Family of the Year" twice, in 1978 and 1979, the only two time winner family. Ann has served on countless tournament committees.

COURTESY CHARLIE COX

Daughter Catherine learning to serve

ANOTHER FIRST FOR CHARLIE

A little more than ten years after the USTA's 1968 creation of "open tennis," Charlie Cox, his fertile mind again at work, came up with another idea. He had envisioned a "senior" professional event for Atlanta, featuring a small number of well known players no longer able to compete with younger players coming into the game, but couldn't find the sponsors to pull it off, and didn't have the time to work on it, between flying for Delta, family obligations, and playing tournaments himself. Cliff Drysdale had encouraged him to stick with it, but he eventually gave up.

And then, eureka, the sponsor he had been unable to find came to him, out of the blue. The International Management Group, a global sports management company, had been working with Carte Blanch Credit Card on the same concept, and wanted to stage the first one in Atlanta.

Cox' name surfaced as a logical contact, and voila, he became the first ever Tournament Director of a "Tennis Legends Championship" event. And what's more, they would pay him.

The year was 1979. He decided an ideal venue would be his alma mater's basketball stadium, the Georgia Tech Coliseum. It would be an eight man event, four sessions played over three days, the last day being the two session one on Saturday. The prize money: $35,000 total. The tickets would be in blocks of four, working out to just under $10 per person per session, and individual day passes as low as $6. The players would be Rod Laver, Ken Rosewall, Roy Emerson, Fred Stolle, John Newcome, Marty Reissen, Tom Okker, and Cliff Drysdale. $35,000. Hmmm. That averages out to about $1500 per player per (three hour max) day, enough to pay for a nice hotel and travel comfortably, but certainly not a windfall.

To put this in perspective, in November 2009, for a one day exhibition event in Prague the sponsor forked over close to $70,000 for each player, for a few over the hill guys, including Boris Becker, Mats Wilander, and Stephan Edberg.

On the porch at
Bitsy Grant Tennis Center

JOE BECKNELL

A natural athlete, his road to becoming a tennis pro was circuitous. A talented musician, he almost pursued a singing career.

He was born in 1938, and was in the first graduating class of newly established Westminster Schools[1] in north Atlanta, and went on to graduate from Mercer, where he played baseball until he injured a knee. He had dreamed of a pro baseball career but the injury changed that, and he switched to tennis, playing two years on the Mercer team, because, in his words *"even though I wasn't much good, the team was not too competitive, so I managed to play regularly at position 5 or 6."*

He went on to teach English and Latin at Fulton High School and later at the Lovett School, and pursued a graduate degree at UGA, in the classics.

A chance meeting with Larry Shippey in 1958 during a ping pong match, the Atlanta City championships, at the Atlanta City Auditorium, led him into a friendship that would change his life. The two met in the finals, and the match was prolonged, each making virtually no errors, and in the tiebreaker, Shippey, in the typical steady, error free play that characterized his tennis, finally prevailed.

Joe at that time was playing tennis, mostly at Piedmont Park on the red clay there. Thunderstorms with hard rain would take all the red clay courts in town out of play for sometimes several days. A friend suggested that Bitsy Grant Tennis Center had state of the art fast draining and drying rubico, at that time a surface found only at private clubs. Wandering in one day, not knowing anyone, Shippey spotted him, and said, *"...I remember you..."* They played a few sets, resulting in a humbled Becknell. He says of that first match with Shippey, *"...all I did was chase the ball...and I thought I could play..."*

COURTESY JOE BECKNELL

The two became fast friends, and Becknell improved so much that in just a few years, in 1966, he became an assistant teaching pro at the center under Head Pro Jack Rogers. He won the Atlanta City singles title in 1968, in the finals defeating Woody Blocher (national boys 16's winner in 1967, later an ATP tour player).

He considers his most memorable victory to be winning the Georgia 35's doubles with former Georgia Tech football coach Bobby Dodd, 68 at the time. A few years later, playing in the Atlanta Invitational, he extended Chuck McKinley, 6 time Davis Cup player and Wimbledon winner only 5 years before, to three sets. He has won 18 Georgia State Singles.

He's held a number of teaching positions including Tennis Director of Atlanta Athletic Club, Cumberland Indoor Tennis Club, Terminus Athletic Club (later Atlanta Health and Racket Club), Northside Athletic Club (now Australian Body Works), and the Carl Sanders YMCA, from which he retired in 2007.

He's dominated every age group in singles in the state rankings, holding down No. 1 from the 35's through the 55's. He's won four national doubles titles with partner John Skogstad, the first in the 50's (humiliating Frank Froeling (No. 6 in the world in 1963)) and partner, 6-0, 6-4), and three in the 55's.

Not bad for a Latin teacher.

See also pp 132, 133

---

[1] *Westminster originated in 1951 as a reorganization and merger of two of Atlanta's most exclusive private schools, the North Avenue Presbyterian School (NAPS) and Washington Seminary. Hence the plural name.*

AL PARKER

THE GREATEST JUNIOR
PLAYER OF ALL TIME

He won more tournaments in the 12's, 14's, 16's and 18's than any other junior player, ever. Today, he's an investment banker in Atlanta who absolutely loves golf and never plays tennis.

During a family trip to Hilton Head, SC, his parents put six year-old Al into a child's tennis clinic so they could have time for some fun mixed doubles with friends. The pro told them he'd never seen a child so gifted. His mother, Sally, decided to start him in lessons, but waited two years. *"A child only gets to be a child once,"* she said *"I had a feeling that once it ever started it would be non-stop."*

She was right. It was non-stop. In 1981, during his second year in the 12 and unders, he won the singles and doubles at all four national tournaments, a double grand slam, the only person in the history of American junior tennis to do that.

Parents, Mid and Sally Parker remember their son as a serious and extremely disciplined child - *"...he was more disciplined than we were..."* He was a perfectionist who made his bed as soon as he was tall enough to reach it. He got A's in every single class he ever took. When he began playing tennis he became obsessed with hitting every ball perfectly and supplemented his lessons by hitting against a wall outside his home every day for hours.

When he began entering local tournaments, he was big for his age, extremely steady from the baseline, and more mentally mature than his peers. *"...I was able to focus better and stay in the match a little bit better than the other kids...I don't know why I had that ability..."* He also hated to lose. *"I don't care if it's tennis, croquet, or whatever,"* Sally said, *"he will get after you with 200%... and make you think you cannot win."*

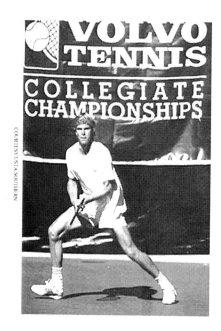

COURTESY USTA SOUTHERN

At nine he won club tournaments, at ten he won Georgia state tournaments, and at eleven he won a 12 and under national in Houston.

In 1987, his last year in the 18s, he won his 25th national and set a record for cumulative national titles. Playing a total of 66 matches as a junior, he won or was a finalist in 38 of them, making his odds of reaching the finals, by just showing up, near 60%. Jim Courier once said, *"...he was larger than life. When the draw showed you were going to play Al, you just booked your flight. OK. It's over. Off to the next tournament."*

He was voted All-American four times while at the University of Georgia. But according to his coach at Georgia, Dan Magill, *"...he almost never practiced. He couldn't. He was always hurt, and in the training room..."*

He had a congenital back problem, spondylolisthesis, that severely limited his tennis career.

At Georgia he was a dedicated student. He maintained a 4.0 grade point average all the way through his four years, to the dismay of Coach Magill, who recalls telling him, *"...you can't stay up all night studying, and then play a tennis match..."* But he did, and almost always won. He graduated Summa Cum Laude.

After graduation, he hit the pro circuit. In two years, he won four Futures events but in Challenger and regular ATP tournaments he often lost in the first or second round, and often to players of lesser ability. His back condition wasn't helped by long flights to places like Kuala Lumpor, Jakarta, and Dubai. Then he tore a rotator cuff. Then stress fractures in a foot. Then shin splints. Then a torn stomach muscle. And along with the physical side, the vagabond lifestyle tarnished the luster of the pro tour.

"I don't know if I ever wanted it bad enough...when you play for your school, and there's thousands of people watching and cheering, its fun,....but when you're on the tour and you're playing a match where 99% of the people live in poverty with no plumbing, you've got three people watching your match, and this guy's serve hits a rock and flies out of the stadium, I say to myself, 'what am I doing here'?"

After two years, he had had enough. He married his high school sweetheart, got his MBA from Harvard, and settled down to business.

He was inducted into the Collegiate, the Georgia, and the Southern Tennis Halls of Fame.

A former coach, Gery Groslimond, sums it up: *"...a lot of guys...who were No. 1 in the world...are not really nice people. They're empty people. Al is nice and well rounded."*

"I don't know if I ever wanted it bad enough...when you play for your school, and there's thousands of people watching... it's fun..."

1978, Crackerland Winner

Al Parker's spectacular junior career seemed to virtually guarantee that he would dominate professional tennis' top levels for many years. It never happened. There may have been more, but two reasons seem clear. One was a physical condition that developed in his college years, making play increasingly difficult. The more significant factor may have been his focus on other life goals. In contrast with many who pursue the dream of professional tennis, Parker seems to have always had other (conflicting and perhaps subliminal) goals in mind. The odyssey of his travels through the junior and collegiate tennis ranks and the ultimate decision to go in another direction was captured and chronicled in an exceptional article appearing in the April 2000 issue of *"Tennis Magazine."* The article is now widely circulated and available to anyone with a computer and access to the internet. Some excerpts:

"...He always wanted to win real bad," Mid (his father) said, *"but when he won he looked like he was embarrassed."* Sally (his mother) said, *"People would always come to me...(and say)* 'is Al upset about anything? Is he not happy that he won'? Because he was very subdued. It wasn't in him ever to gloat."* To that question, Al would reply, *'The biggest thing for me was to never rub it in anybody's face.'* Gery Groslimond, his coach throughout the juniors, described him as *'..maybe the most normal national champion of all time... He reminded me a lot of Rod Laver in terms of character...'*

After matches the Parkers' van was the place to be. *"That family was just so loving,"* Murphy Jensen said. *"...they were just a great tennis family."*

At fifteen he shot up six inches to six-foot-three in a handful of months and lost his coordination. He served entire matches underhand. And there were more mental problems. *"I definitely felt like I was tired mentally,"* he said. *"It had been intense since I was 12 and over time that takes a toll... I definitely felt like I was tired by the time I was 16. Tired mentally. And some of that translates to physical. I was tired before I got to the part where I was gonna be makin money playing."*

At 18 there was a fork in the road: move on to college or go on the tour? At that point it was still uncommon for Americans to skip college completely... Many people told Parker he should skip college but he didn't consider it. *"I was pretty focused on doin' college and doin' it at Georgia."* he said...He decided on a finance major and earned a 4.0. *"He would stay up so late I used to cuss him out,"* said Dan Magill, his coach...*'I said you gon' lose a match for Georgia for you stayin' up all night studying'* He also joined a fraternity and had a rich social life. *"Girls loved the guy,"* Jim Childs said. *"We would trail Al around town. Let him be the lead guy, we would be his wing men..."* *"In college your apartment's supposed to be a wreck,"* said friend and fellow player Wade McGuire, *"but in his room everything would be perfect. You go into his closet, everything was perfectly lined up. You open his desk drawer and the tacks would all be in order."*

He won his first two collegiate tournaments. But in his third, the SEC Indoors at the University of Alabama, when he stretched for a ball, he felt a strange tweak in his back. As the match went on it turned into serious pain.. Back at Georgia the doctor discovered he had spondylolisthesis, a condition that causes discs in the lower spine to push on one another and cause tremendous pain. In Parker's case, one of his discs was cracked. *"But I was still able to perform at a high level even with the back..."*

His last three years at Georgia Parker won two big tournaments and got straight A's.
"That 4.0 was of the utmost importance to him," said Manuel Diaz, Georgia's head coach Parker's last three years...he graduated Summa Cum Laude and was named the Academic All-American for all sports.

In the summer of 1991 Parker hit the pro tour. His back was aggravated by long flights...He won four satellite tournaments but in Challenger and ATP events he usually lost in the first or second round, often to players of lesser ability... *"I was just continuously injured,"* he said. His body was falling apart...

At Georgia he had his teammates and coaches. In the pros he had no one. The reasons why he wanted to win escaped him. *"...In the juniors and college I wanted to win bad... I was into it for reasons other than just internally wanting to win... you're playing for your team and for the school and there's 5,000 people watching. One day I was in Bangalore... there's three people watching and nobody cares and this guy's serve hits a rock on the court and rockets out of the stadium and I'm saying to myself, what am I doin' here?"*

One blistering hot day at a tournament in Texas, with Mid in the crowd, Al lost to a lesser player. He walked off and said, *"Dad, this is not working out. I think I'm gonna quit."* Mid told him, *"Buddy, I concur with ya 100%."* *"We all breathed a collective sigh of relief,"* Sally said.

"He never seemed to be the least bit depressed," Sally said. *"Now, I've heard him say 'it's kinda hard to watch these guys out there doin so great,' and he wonders why didn't it work out for him, but he doesn't brood about it. He's busy with what he's doin' now. And I'm so thankful that all of this did not take a negative toll on him because I think it could've destroyed somebody. I really do think it had that potential."*

Gery Groslimond: *"There's a lot of guys who were number one in the world and they're not really nice people or they're empty people. He's well-rounded. He's very happy today and I don't know if a lot of players who are number one in the world can say that after their playing days are over. Or even while they're number one."*

Parker said he has no regrets. *"Certainly I think about what it might've been like if I was a top player in the world, but I've moved on from it. It does not bother me. I don't ever look back at my tennis career with any sort of bad feelings because I couldn't be happier with what I'm doing today. I enjoy my career, I enjoy my family, I enjoy the fact that I'm not still out there trying to grind through injury problems on the tour. I love my life and I'm incredibly happy, and happy for those guys."*

In the scheme of life, it doesn't matter that the greyhounds overtook him because Parker made something of his life. The game's great gift to him—unimaginable early success—became a curse, but the measure of character is not the peaks you reach, it's the valleys from which you escape... *"I wouldn't say his life is incomplete because he didn't make it on the tour,"* Courier said. *"I shudder to think that you throw all your eggs of happiness in the basket of tennis."*

Nowadays he can't serve two games without tremendous pain; he doesn't watch tennis on television because he'd rather play with his son or hit the links; and he almost never discusses his past.

"Occasionally I'll have a meeting with a client who'll recognize my name or something and everyone else from my firm will be like, 'what, you used to play tennis'?"

WENDY WHITE PRAUSA

She's the only WTA player to have turned pro while in college and still graduate on time.

Her tennis began at summer camp as an 8 year old. She became a dominant junior player in Georgia, and between 1977 and 1978 she won or was a finalist in more than 30 tournaments. She won the Regional AA Georgia State High School singles four years running, 1975 through 1978, and in 1978 received a full scholarship to Rollins College. She was ranked nationally No. 8 in the Girl's 18's in 1978. In 1980, she was named Collegiate Player of the Year by Tennis Magazine. She played on the Junior Wightman Cup team for the U.S. in 1977 and 1978, and the WTA tour from 1978 until 1990, reaching the quarters of the US Open doubles twice.

COURTESY SOUTHERN TENNIS ASSOCIATION

Her highest ranking as a pro was No. 18, in 1982. A versatile all-court player, she had wins over some of the game's legends, including two against Billie Jean King. The U.S. Professional Tennis Registry recognized her as the Player of the Decade in 2000, and the following year she was inducted into the Southern and the Georgia Tennis Halls of Fame.

RANDY STEPHENS

A leader of the tennis community in Macon, Georgia, Randy has been an active playing and teaching professional for many years. He's been ranked as high as No. 2 nationally in both the Men's Open and Mixed doubles.

He has served in the Southern Professional Tennis Association (two terms as president) and as president of the Georgia Professional Tennis Association and as president of the Southern, the Georgia, and the Macon Tennis Associations. In 2004, he was honored for his service to the game with the presentation of the USTA Southern Section's Charlie B. Morris Award. He has won both the Georgia and Southern Tennis Professional of the Year awards, the Pride of the South Award (USPTA/Southern), and the John Drew Smith Memorial Award (Macon Tennis Association)

He is employed by Smith Barney as a Financial and Retirement Planning Consultant.

COURTESY RANDY STEPHENS

JERRY CALDWELL

Caldwell, of Madison, Georgia, is one of those players where during the warmup before a match, an opponent might be elated when looking across the net to see what looks like a beginner, with awkward and unconventional strokes. And then get his brains knocked out on the court.

His style is self-taught; the stories about it are legion. To many players who have less than perfect form, he's a hero. Some jokingly say he's an example of how not to hit a tennis ball.

A natural doubles player, he has been ranked nationally in the top 5 many times. In 1981 he held three Southern section doubles rankings, Nos. 1, 2, and 3, with three different partners. He's made his mark in singles also, once No. 1 nationally in his age group, 10 times as No. 1 in the Southern section, 15 times in Georgia.

A talented athlete, he played baseball and basketball in high school, and talked his coach into letting him squeeze in tennis in his senior year.

COURTESY SOUTHERN TENNIS ASSOCIATION

He won the city's high school doubles championship in his first tournament. At Vanderbilt University he played both varsity basketball and baseball, and there was no squeezing for tennis at that level, so he played only intramural tennis, and a few tournaments during the summer.

His mark in tennis came late in life. In 1986, he won the USTA National Men's 45's Clay Doubles and has been a national doubles finalist 11 times. He's won many Georgia and Southern Section championships.

COURTESY BITSY GRANT TENNIS ASSOCIATION

JACK TEAGLE

One of the oldest pictures at Bitsy Grant Tennis Center is of a player who figured prominently among the very best, based on newspaper clippings from the '30's and '40's, as either a winner or finalist in many tournaments, with almost no additional information beyond his name.

Players now in their 80's will remember his very distinctive style; he sliced every ball on either side.

ARMISTEAD C. NEELY
SATELLITE PIONEER

Many recreational players are only vaguely aware of tennis' minor leagues.

The International Tennis Federation listed 53 events on their schedule for August 2010, a typical month; only one, in Decatur IL, was in the USA. The rest were in far away places like Novi Sad, Serbia, or Na-korn-Ratchaisima, Thailand, and many offer "prize money" of no more than $5000 total, meaning a lot of players don't come close to making expenses. But there are legions of skilled players, many with regular day jobs, who play in them. For several reasons; one is "points," which enable one to gain entry into bigger events where the money is serious; and they get to keep playing at a high level with the chance of earning something, however small it may be.

Forty years ago it was worse. Second tier tournaments offered even less money and no point system for entry into larger events.

Enter Mssrs. Neely and friend Larry Turville. They crafted something they called the WATCh circuit (World Association of Tennis Champions). Not only put it together, they ran it, on a shoe string budget. And it worked, for 7 years, usually 10 events, all in Florida, with prize money as much as ten times the then going rate, and pulled it off with innovations like private home housing in exchange for tennis clinics and pro-ams. Spectators loved it, the 300 or so players from 30 different countries loved it, and enthusiastic volunteers worked for nothing to put the tournament on.

The dark side was, the circuit eclipsed other available events; the USTA viewed them as troublesome and refused to sanction them. Ultimately, and sadly, the exhausted founders turned the operation over to the USTA and it lost its unique character, but positive changes resulted.

COURTESY ARMISTEAD NEELY

Ironically, the USTA recognized genius and Neely became the USTA Satellite Tournament Director in the years following, 1982 and 1983.

Neely's performance in junior and collegiate tennis (University of Florida) was outstanding, followed by a successful professional career both as a player and later in college coaching, tournament directing and as tennis director at various clubs.

Listing all his titles would require several pages, single spaced. That he's won 25 gold balls (for winning a national USTA event) and 21 silver balls (for being in the finals) says it all.

But he regards his role in conceiving, implementing and shaping the format of early satellite events as his proudest achievement in tennis.

"Had it not been for my mother Peggy, I might have just hung out at the rec center in front of our apartment in Tampa and never picked up a racket. She had never played but thought my friends at the center were 'rough.' She hauled me off to the Davis Island Tennis Center, where I could meet 'nice' children.   I was 8.

"I started taking lessons from the pro there, using a racket someone gave me, a 30 year old wooden monster, twice as heavy as today's adult rackets. I liked all sports, and found I had a feel for tennis, and by age eleven I had a national ranking and was being driven all over Florida to tournaments by my mother. My father had played a little tennis growing up, but his interest at first was mild. He didn't participate in the tournament driving, and rarely watched any of my matches, but he enjoyed hanging out at the tennis center, and after a while he was spending all his free time there, and was stringing rackets for all my friends. He became great friends with everyone there and it became a social outlet for him.

"Money for getting to and playing in tournaments was always a problem. When I was 9, I got the job of cleaning up around the center and stocking the drink machine; I earned fifty cents an hour. I kept that job for the next 7 years, and they were paying my father to do various things around the courts. Between what he earned and I earned, we had enough to pay for my court time. I was able to play in the National Juniors in Kalamazoo, for several years, only because I was named to the Junior Davis Cup team and got financial support from the USTA to pay travel expenses. I never won the tournament there, but was ranked No. 2 nationally in the 16's, and the last year I played, in the 18's, I had three match points in a three setter against Stan Smith in the quarters, but he eventually pulled it out."

Armistead Neely, 2009

BRANCH CURRINGTON

A 13 year old Branch began working at the Piedmont Driving Club in Atlanta, long a bastion of wealth and privilege, white only except for employees. He was employed as an assistant in the tennis maintenance department, preparing courts for play, and as a as a 'ball boy.'

Today you see them a lot on televised matches. Its a position of honor, and speeds up play for the benefit of spectators and the media. But other than at big tournaments, they are an anachronism, a vestige of an era gone by. At the Driving Club, they got paid, and it was good money for the lucky ones.

In the 20's and 30's, participation in the sport demanded appropriate convenience for the ladies and gentlemen playing, and properly maintained conditions, the red clay courts carefully watered, rolled, the lines carefully marked with chalk (actually an altered version of ordinary lime known then as 'improved whitening,' which maintains its shape after drying, not cracking as ordinary lime would), towels and water at the ready, and small boys whose duty was to scamper around and retrieve errant balls and deliver them to the players.

In the process, he learned, and his fascination with the game grew. With the gift of a battered racket by a club member and a few discarded balls, he began, in his off time, to play his own version of the game, hitting balls against a schoolhouse wall, despite taunts by peers, who labeled tennis, and him, as "*sissy.*"

COURTESY BRANCH CURRINGTON

WWII service in the army gave him an opportunity for a regular paycheck, to help his family. He enlisted.

When he came back, the Driving Club had hired a pro, Welby Van Horn, at the time one of a small handful of tennis professionals with national recognition, to enhance the tennis program at the club. Van Horn taught him the finer points of tennis club operation, including racket stringing; and, when time permitted, the fundamentals of stroke production and how to teach.

He became a competent player and teacher, and when Van Horn was not available, he would occasionally give instruction to members. An opportunity for advancement occurred when he was promoted to take the place of an older co-worker on the tennis staff, Sammy Lindsey, who had moved up to become "Head Doorman," at the club; but not much changed.

Van Horn advised him, if he wanted a career in tennis to go north or west, But thoughts of leaving family, children, and aging parents prevailed.

He left tennis.

As assistant tennis pro at the
Piedmont Driving Club
ca 1950

With a family to support, he found himself pumping gas, selling groceries, at one point running a restaurant, and then a door-to-door salesman of bed sheets. He bought them from a wholesaler in downtown Atlanta, 1000 at a time, for .25 each, and sold them for $2.50 each, .25 down and .25 a week, and made his rounds weekly to collect the .25 payments, one at a time. After a time, razor blades and other products were added.

After he survived this way for a few years, the Atlanta City Recreation department decided, out of the blue, to hire a tennis professional at its newly renovated Washington Park courts, and in deference to the designation in 1919 of the park as a place for blacks, the pro had to be African American. Branch was well known, and an obvious choice. The park had been donated to the city by early 20th century African American developer Herman Perry, starting with 6 acres, and expanding to 25 acres when completed in 1928. It included a swimming pool, a dance hall, and a pavilion, in addition to the tennis courts. To say he was "hired" was a stretch; it was $50 a month, and whatever he could eke out by his wits, giving lessons, stringing rackets, and selling clothing and food. But it was an open door, and a return to tennis. But not the tennis he had become accustomed to. The clientele was enthusiastic, but poor. Most of his revenue came not from lessons, but from selling crackers, hot dogs and cokes, and some from balls (mostly used, many scrounged from the Driving Club courts) and stringing.

He was the first African American in Georgia to become a certified teaching professional. As his reputation as a teacher grew, he slowly built a more affluent clientele, many of them white, coming from downtown on their lunch hour for a lesson, and through resourcefulness he found niches beyond lessons, hot dogs, and the park. One of these was racket stringing. At his high point, tennis shops far away were shipping their stringing jobs to him, by mail and greyhound bus. He had established connections with several racket manufacturers, and stringing was bringing in more than all his other sources combined. Success inevitably brings competition, and as others moved in, his outside stringing income faded, but by that time he had built up his teaching revenue, affording him the luxury of doing what he wanted to do, teaching tennis to those who could not afford to pay anything.

He made it work for the next 28 years.

In his office at home, 2009

Photo by the author

"...My high school math teacher...worked with us as our tennis coach. Branch Currington was one of the better players (at Washington Park)... I watched in awe when he served...the ball seemed to stop and wait for him. ...as a teenager, (he) had worked at the Piedmont Driving Club, watering, dragging the courts...every day. .. younger blacks worked there as ball boys. That's how we got most of our tennis balls at Washington Park...Branch picked up the game, and after a few years he was giving lessons to Driving Club members..."

Marvin Arrington, "Making My Mark"

COURTESY BRANCH CURRINGTON

With Atlanta City Councilman (and now Judge) Marvin Arrington (far left) and Atlanta Mayor Andrew Young, with camera, ca 1985

"I identified his house by the two blue Dodge vans he told me would be in the driveway. He's lived in the small brick ranch house near Atlanta's airport for 30 years.

"Now alone, he was married for near 30 years before his wife passed away. I asked why two cars? 'I had a Lexus, but you know you have to use premium gas in those, so I sold it, and bought these two cars...'Why two? 'Well, you know, my grandchildren now and then need to borrow one.'

"He has a weekly routine of going to lunch with one of them every Thursday, and taking her home. She attends Woodward Academy. A private school? That's expensive isn't it? 'Well, you do what you have to do. Its a good school, and that's what they need in today's world. I don't want them to have to struggle like I did.'

"Struggle" is an understatement. He had grown up in Atlanta's 'Pittsburgh' community, with little education, but a strong sense of family and good parents. Today he lives alone, the house comfortable, neat, and spotless, not one typical of a bachelor lifestyle.

"One bedroom is his office, pictures lining all the walls, many of family, and dozens of politicians and civic leaders with whom he has had contact,

and certificates of various awards for his public service through the years. They speak silently of his stature in the community.

"The older images show a strikingly handsome figure, stylishly dressed, in either tennis whites or coat and tie.

"His appearance alone would open many doors. His personal grooming has not changed. Now in his late eighties, he moves with a dignity, grace and agility that belies his years.

"That Branch Currington was able to carve out a life in tennis is a near miracle. It happened almost by accident. He was one of 8 children in a poor family. His father was a jack of all trades, sometimes a carpenter when he could find work, and a part time minister.

"An army of children have passed through his courtside classroom, learning not only tennis but the lessons of life. He later became tennis coach for Clark College, now Clark Atlanta University, one of the founding members of the Southeastern Intercollegiate Athletic Conference, formed in 1913 for intercollegiate athletics among black colleges in the southeast."

"Branch no longer teaches, but his style was apparent in a discussion of today's youthful preoccupations with things that lead nowhere. We stopped at an intersection and watched as a young boy in front of us clung to his saggy pants to keep them from falling. It drew a murmur and he volunteered that he had never allowed ball caps to be worn backwards. 'Unless you want to go home.'

"We somehow got on the subject of a well-known nemesis of teaching pros, smitten female students who make advances. Male athletic prowess has been a turn on for females since time began, and part of giving lessons involves being up close and personal. He acknowledged it, and developed a strategy to fend them off. He related one incident involving a young lady whose agenda was visiting the tennis shop daily on the pretense of buying tennis clothes, in addition to weekly lessons. The ruse was transparent; he did not fall for it, and she became discouraged and went elsewhere.

"Perhaps his greatest success story was Horace Reid, who played at UCLA and later successfully on the ATP. Given the normal progression of junior players in today's world, that Reid would be developed by a coach with limited resources and win at Kalamazoo is incredible, but it happened.

"I asked at one point in our conversation how many had gone on to tennis scholarships, and his answer, "49," was so quick that it left no doubt about his sense of pride in it.

"As we discussed various things, I kept waiting for some hint of bitterness, a flicker of resentment, some discontent or criticism of his former all white employers at the Driving Club. It never came. Moreover, his deep affection and respect for many of them, even now, years later, was apparent, and clearly genuine; '...Is ___ still around? Ever see him? He was a gentleman, always a smart dresser...'

"The closest he came was describing the eccentricities of some. '...Mr. Grant, now he was particular about stringing. When I would do a racket for him, I would cross my fingers and hope nothing broke when he started playing with the one I had just done, before I left for the day'

"One of the oddities of the courts at the Driving Club is a deviation in court orientation, because of space limitations. Normally, courts are placed roughly north-south, or better, 22 degrees west of north, recommended by the USTA, which gives right handed servers less sun in their eyes in the winter months. The Driving Club courts ran, of necessity, parallel to Piedmont Avenue. This abnormality was solved by a semi-annual 90 degree rotation of the courts, involving lifting the net posts and re-setting them, and re-setting the lines, covering the old net post sleeves with a cap and clay. As I listened open-mouthed at this anecdote, he explained, with a sly grin and a chuckle, a twinkle in his eye, '...can't have a white man suffering trying to play with sun in his eyes, now, can we?'

"There was no malice in this comment, only humor. Branch Currington has the right stuff. "

Author, 2010

EDDIE WILLLMSON
TENNIS IN THE GEORGIA OUTBACK - THE "THRILLA' IN CAMILLA"

COURTESY EDDIE WILLIAMSON

"Where did you say the tournament is? What's that, Camilla? Never heard of it - - what's it close to?"

Eddie Williamson and wife Nan moved to Camilla over 35 years ago. An innovative, persuasive and successful salesman (and ex-college tennis player, Auburn), Eddie has been a force in almost all community activities, president of many of them. He hatched an idea to undertake what many would say is a long shot - get top tennis professionals to travel from (mostly) big cities and put on a show, without paying them. He had to work with a mix of a little and a lot - the "little" being the six public courts of the Mitchell County Tennis Center, a long way from big cities, the "lot" being an enthusiastic tennis community that became captivated with the idea, and opened their homes to participants as houseguests, reminiscent of the days before open tennis, and domination by professionals expecting big bucks. They don't play a match and go back to a motel. They play, then go a party, and then to a private home and a family.

It caught on, evolved as a social happening, and has been running now for over 34 years. A lucky hand full of Georgia pros get a taste of tennis mixed with constant parties, gourmet cooking, small town hospitality and southern gentility, where winning is good but not everything, and have been coming back for years. They get the royal treatment from local residents, with low-country boils and barbeques, and the local Dairy Queen serves up "blizzards" to players (on Eddie's tab). Members of the community come out to participate in free clinics and enjoy top-level tennis during the pro/am exhibition. They call it the Mitchell County Pro Invitational, a charity event, raising funds for an array of organizations including the Boys and Girls Clubs of Mitchell County, the Mitchell-Baker Service Center (for physically and mentally handicapped), the Southwest Georgia pro Technical College, and the Mitchell County Food Bank.

Southwest Georgia in the first half of the 20th century, after rail transportation penetrated the area, became a millionaire's winter playground, with mega-plantations of 20,000 acres abounding, most dedicated to pursuit of the state game bird, the Bobwhite Quail, in the grand style, with morning and afternoon hunts, white coated dog handlers, mule drawn wagons, mint juleps and garden parties for those on the social register.

That era has largely passed, and many plantations have become commercialized or broken into smaller tracts, and many of the antebellum homes converted to B&B's, but the magic of the area, the mild climate, tall pines, wildlife and wiregrass are still there. Hoagy Carmichael nailed it when he penned the lyrics, and singer Ray Charles immortalized it; *"Georgia, Georgia...sweet and clear..., as moonlight through the pines..."*.

To date, over $1,000,000 has been raised. Donations come from the $150 per person entry fee and 15 local corporate sponsors that make donations of up to $5,000 each. *"We are the only center (Mitchell-Baker Service Center) in the state of Georgia that was not paid for with government money..."*

Sponsors took some selling initially; now they line up to be part of the action, and hundreds of individuals and families pay a minimum of $75 to have their name listed.

The event has given tennis in the area a huge shot in the arm. Williamson petitioned the County Commissioners for junior tennis program funding, and the courts are now filled with over 150 kids who participate in clinics and leagues each week.

"When you mention Camilla, thousands in the tennis world know (about it) because of Eddie," said USTA Southern Section Executive Director John Callen.

Tournament partiers holding off the rain

"He has raised hundreds of thousands of dollars for charities with the tennis event that has become the social event of the year in Camilla."

Eddie Williamson was inducted into the Georgia Hall of Fame in 2006 after the tournament earned a record $50,000 in charitable donations.

The USTA recognized Williamson with the 2006 Seniors' Service Award for the impact his efforts have had on the community and tennis.

"Once you come to Camilla, you want to keep going back because of the great competition and lasting friendships made while helping an incredible charity in a 'one-stop light' town," said Roy Barth. *"It shows you how much one person can do in a small community. Tennis needs more people like Eddie Williamson."*

Atlanta pro Armistead Neely, playing in the "Thrilla"

THE HOWELLS OF ATLANTA
SOUTHERN TENNIS ASSOCIATION'S TENNIS FAMILY OF THE YEAR

On the court at home
Left to right Jimbo, Peter, Richard, Speed, Arthur, Carrie, Lindy, and Eleanor

George Arthur Howell

"*I played football, basketball and tennis at Princeton; but in my freshman year, I tore the heck out of my knee playing football against Pennsylvania, and that ended my career as far as being a serious amateur tennis player. I could still move enough to play doubles, and I won a lot of things with my wife, my sons, and my daughters. And it was just iced tea, nothing more.*"

Arthur Howell, 2009

Arthur and Carrie Howell produced a platoon of talented tennis players, and their collective trophies would require a large ballroom to display.

Arthur's family's Atlanta footprints go back several generations. One physical monument still exists in Atlanta, the venerable Neel Reid designed Hass-Howell building at 75 Poplar St., built to house his father's insurance firm, now surviving as the prestigious Haas and Dodd Agency.

That firm was for many years intertwined with the Coca-Cola Company. Arthur chose the law instead of insurance, and in 1958, his firm merged with that of golfing legend Bobby Jones, becoming Jones, Bird & Howell, now surviving as Alston & Bird, one of the country's largest. The Howell-Jones friendship endured near fifty years, until Jones' death in 1971. Howell represented Jones, as a lawyer for a lawyer, for years, in connection with Jones' substantial Coke interests.

From whence, perhaps, comes his strong preference for amateur sports. His colleague Jones had said many times, "*...its just a game...*"

114

RICHARD HOWELL achieved stardom at each phase of life, moving from star junior to star collegiate to star adult tennis player to well known lawyer to sports agent.

He formed Robinson Humphrey Sports Enterprises in 1985, took it private in 1986, and built it into national prominence in the field. Their tennis clients have included Michael Pernfors and Bryan Shelton. National notoriety came with the epic and prolonged negotiations with the Dallas Cowboys and owner Jerry Jones to land a record breaking contract for superstar Emmitt Smith.

He served as president of the Georgia Tennis Association from 1984 to 1985, and was inducted into the Georgia Tennis Hall of Fame in 1985.

Above, Richard Howell, left, with Henry Feild, Crackerland Tournament Athens, Ga.

Field would later play No. 1 singles for UGA 1964-1966 and would captain the tennis team. His untimely death in a 1968 car crash prompted the University of Georgia to name the UGA stadium in his honor.

Above left, Lindy on the steps at Bitsy; right, Eleanor, with companions

ELEANOR: *"I played ALTA with Mother as my partner for quite a few years, and once after we won our match, one of our opponents asked, '...why do you keep calling your partner 'Mother?'*
I said, 'because she's my mother.'
She was 79 at the time."

"In our last ALTA season together my mother elected to go on another team 'where she could be a star.'

"I missed playing with her, but we were at different levels by this time. She was hampered by her COPD, and it was amazing that she could play tennis at all, because she was on oxygen off of the court. Toward the end, my mother did not warm up. She didn't want to waste any energy.

"I have fond memories of going down to Bitsy on Sunday mornings when my parents played mixed doubles against each other, Mother with Don Smith, and Dad with Natalie Cohen. We had to take the playpen for Jimbo, who was born in 1952."

LINDY: *"Eleanor and I won the sister-sister tournament at Bitsy back when we were in high school. That trophy is my favorite. I won the Georgia State Closed at Bitsy, beating both my former high school doubles partner and my sister, when I was in my last year in the Juniors and was able to go to the Jaycees at Wichata, Kansas, but Ethel Robertson and I lost in the first round. One of my favorite memories is being down 5-0 in the third set of a match at Bitsy and then winning seven straight games for victory. I learned a hard lesson in another match one time at Bitsy; it started raining, and during the delay my opponent remembered the score differently than I did. I lost."*

BOYS' SINGLES

1. Harry Thompson, III............................Atlanta, Ga.
2. Spencer Allen...................................Atlanta, Ga.
3. Ned Neely.......................................Atlanta, Ga.
4. Chuck Tuller....................................Atlanta, Ga.
5. James Tarr......................................Louisville, Ky.
6. Steve Stephenson................................Atlanta, Ga.
7. John Robinson...................................Baton Rouge, La.
8. Max Gartman.....................................Mobile, Ala.
9. Stu McCloy......................................Memphis, Tenn.
10. Walker Lockett.................................Greensboro, N. C.
11. Gray Smith.....................................Nashville, Tenn.
12. Ben Keyes......................................Greenville, S. C.

Above, the Southern Tennis Association Boys 15 and under 1954 rankings

1951 Westminster team, front L-R Harry Thompson, Ivan Allen III, Ned Neely, Charles Tuller; rear, Tread Davis, Westminster Coach Jack Waters, Spencer Allen

Vienna, Georgia

Georgia Tech Coach Earl Bortell

THE GEORGIA TENNIS
HALL OF FAME MUSEUM

at the time of its dedication at Bitsy Grant Tennis Center, January 2009
Photo by the author

The large trophy in the center of the room, displayed courtesy of Mary Grant Macdonald, is inscribed with winners of the United States Lawn Tennis Association National Clay Court Championships from 1927 until 1935. It was retired in 1935 after Bitsy's third win.   Past Winners were, 1927 William Tilden; 1929 Emmett Pare (there was no tournament in 1928); 1930 Bryan Grant; 1931 H.E. Vines; 1932 George Lott, Jr.; 1933 Frank Parker; 1934 Bryan Grant; 1935 Bryan Grant. The museum has been relocated, and is no longer at Bitsy Grant Tennis Center.

BITSY GRANT TENNIS ASSOCIATION SCRAPBOOKS

The Bitsy Grant Tennis Association kept newspaper clippings and pictures taken over many years, some displayed on a wall leading down the steps of the center to the locker rooms, and some simply mounted in scrapbooks kept at the center. In 2010, most of the pictures and clippings in the dilapidated scrapbooks and on the wall were removed and digitally scanned for preservation. Here are a few:

Jack Mooney

Sara Comer

Harry Gault

Carleton Y. Smith

John Ager

Marjorie Waite Bird

Jim Winstead

Camilla Smith

Betty Braselton

Inez Long

Louise Camp Gibson

Pinky Ager

J. W. Caldwell

Etta Coyne

Zahner Reynolds

BITSY GRANT TENNIS ASSOCIATION
SCRAPBOOKS

WHEN THE WATER WAS CUT OFF

In 2005, Atlanta suffered a drought, and the resulting water crisis prompted the City to cut off the water supply to the Bitsy Grant courts. The Bitsy Grant Tennis Association responded by raising money and drilling a well, saving the day.

A GOOD HAIRDAY

In the '50's and '60's, the center was the venue for many tournaments. Right is Brazilian player Tomas Koch, after his 1969 win of the Atlanta Invitational. Pro Jack Rodgers remarked that his shoulder length hair was *the longest of any player he had ever seen play in the tournament.* Koch's reply was, *"...it just feels like me..."* Had Rodgers been able to look into the future, he might have been shocked to see what was to come—Gael Monfils' "just fell out'a bed" coiffure; Agassi's flowing locks almost down to his waist; John McEnroe, with his white afro; James Blake in his dreadlock phase, and countless others. All make Koch's style look pretty button down. Apparently the gallery had more vision; Rogers reported a huge demand for the headbands worn by Koch, right, during the tournament.

RESURRECTION
The Tree Bar centerpiece is re-planted, thanks to Trees Atlanta, when the landmark white oak passed away in 1991.

Left, Phil Slotin, a Bitsy regular for years and a talented photographer who captured many of the images on these pages.

Below, septuagenarian Natalie Cohen multi-tasking, chairing a match and, with stocking foot resting on the netcord, acting as a net judge. A familiar site at many Atlanta tournaments.

KONG CHU

He's not in any record books, but any regular player at Bitsy Grant Tennis Center knows him. Very few, however, know the connection between the tuxedoed young man in his twenties at left, and how he became the man on the right, an American citizen, a distinguished professor at Georgia Tech, a world lecturer, and a regular at Bitsy Grant Tennis Center. Between the two is an unbelievable WW II odyssey of swimming rivers and dodging bombs, bullets and soldiers. He was born in China in 1926 to highly educated, upper class, cultured parents who both taught school. His father, once runner-up in the Chinese National Championships, taught him to play tennis. China during his youth was in turmoil, the Ching Dynasty having ended in 1911. When Japan seized Manchuria, and began bombing its cities, the family, his parents and his younger brother, to escape the bombing, fled on a fishing boat to the British settlement in Shanghai along the Sowchow River, where they remained until both brothers finished St. Johns Senior Middle School, shortly after the bombing of Pearl Harbor. Part of the journey was by steamboat to Wuhan, where Japanese boarded the ship. Chu and his friends escaped by jumping into the water and hiding in the reeds on the shoreline, eventually crossing a mountain range and reaching Bantung, and from there 400 miles across mountains to Chungking in free China, on foot, sleeping where they could and foraging for food. His fascinating story can be read at http://thestoryofchu.blogspot.com/ .

Danny Lobel, Christmas party host extraordinaire', and friends. The parties were held from 1988 through 1992 at his place of business, Central Electric, on Ponce de Leon Ave.

A PUERTO RICAN RACKET DANCE
Jeannette Honore' performs on the porch

Bitsy regular Pinky Bowers

The Botch's, with Ruth Lay, center, at the
Georgia Tennis Hall of Fame dedication 2009

Mike Bernard and his perennial group have been
playing regularly since the '80's.

L-R Shippey, Stan Smith, Foots (Dr. Glenn) Dudley at a Lobel Christmas Party amidst the lighting displays at Central Electric Company on Ponce de Leon Ave., in Atlanta

Hugh Manning

Bitsy Pro Bailey Brown

L-R Mark Phillips, Bill Wiesen, Stew Lowengrub, Foots Dudley, Larry Shippey

Berry Grant, Linda Baker, and Ken Woods, Friends of
Tennis Dinner, 2003, 50th Anniversary of
Bitsy Grant Tennis Center

Danny Lobel with daughter Robyn

In honor of fallen court warriors.

Peter Howell introduces Director Dersch of the City of Atlanta, re-opening ceremony 2006

Architect Tony Aeck, Mark Walker, Mel Locklear

Right, Bitsyland
String Band, 2007
Summer Social

128

L-R regular tournament player George Kuchenmeister (aka "the cookiemonster"),
Frank Cairns, Danny Lobel, Dan Lyon

Cholly Cup players, 2006

2007 Summer Social: Jack Kelleher, Jim Kennedy, Peter Howell, Sonny McAdoo

Above, Tom Bird, Bitsy regular and holder of multiple national championships,
digs one out playing on the grass at the Newport Casino in 1967

HATTIE GRANT

Great nephew Beau Grant honored his grandfather's sister with this eulogy May 28, 2011 on her passing at age 98; re-printed here in part:

"Harriet Key "Hattie" Grant, 98, passed away...at Wesley Woods' Budd Terrace in Atlanta on Thursday, May 26, 2011.

"Hattie was born October 10, 1912...and attended...Girls High in Atlanta, GA and Hollins College in Roanoke, VA. ...(She was)An Atlanta debutante...the great-granddaughter of Lemuel Grant, who... Transformed...'Marthasville' into a major rail hub now known as Atlanta...

"She served Atlanta tirelessly as a long-standing member of the Junior League... (and)... survived many friends who perished in the plane crash at Paris-Orly Airport, having bowed out of the trip herself for family reasons...

"Among her favorite things was the club sandwich in the Piedmont Driving Club's Park Room...and her second favorite must have been Sunday brunch in the Ball Room with her great nephew, Beau.

"She cooked for her brother (Bitsy), nephew, and great-nephew, all of whom lived with her for many years. Hattie considered all of the Grants her children and made sacrifices for them all...she lived by her own rules, and she was loved by everyone without reserve."

"WHY I QUIT PLAYING TENNIS... IT WAS BECAUSE I COULDN'T BRUSH MY TEETH..."

"Coach Dodd was...the primary reason... I fell in love with Bitsy Grant Tennis Center... and was there by 3 pm weekdays, and by 10 in the morning on weekends. The cast of characters rarely changed. There was the late Bitsy Grant himself, a former world class player, usually with no shirt on, running somebody half to death from one side of the court to the other; then there were Larry, Hank, Tom, and other nationally ranked seniors; and Mark and Chu and Joe and Pinky and Stiles, and Lord knows how many days, Coach Dodd.

"What made Dodd a winner in football, tennis and any other game was that he understood that winning - not how you looked, was the important thing. He had terrible strokes; a two handed scoop lob, and his serve wouldn't break a window pane. But he could land them on a dime.

"A friend and I played Dodd and his son maybe a hundred times, and maybe we split 50 - 50. How they did it was, Coach played the forehand, and 70 percent of the time he would lob his return over the net man. If the sun were in their eyes, it went to 99%. Coach played about a quarter of the court. Anything far left, he would say to Bobby Jr., 'take it brother...' Bobby Jr had a top spin forehand we called the "buzzball." It would start at your head and land at your feet To beat them you had to hit 10 million overheads. I waked up one morning and couldn't brush my teeth because my shoulder hurt."

Lewis Grizzard

BITSY GRANT TENNIS CENTER (1953-2003)…"MEM☺RIES" by Joe Becknell

Just what was it like in those early years, the '50s and '60s, as the BGTC "flourished?"…You had to be there…quite an unbelievable place…nothing like it before or since…those fantastic "ol' Seniors" with their wooden rackets and white tennis balls…the 2-3+ hour waiting lists on the weekends, every weekend…the best tennis players in Atlanta, seniors, men, women, boys, girls…a time before ALT A …before USTA…before "open" tennis…the bleachers by court 1, where the kibitzers constantly took up venue (playing on court 1 was not for the "thin-skinned" or "faint-of-heart")…Ralph Foster, his class and finesse at handling the "disgruntled" as well as the "gruntled" players, and the uncanny wit and wisdom accompanying his zany antics as he ran the Pro Shop and the courts, calling out when a court time was up, "On court 1, your time has "elapsed"--or "On court 3, your time has "expired!"… and, Ralph explaining how he kept getting "jumpers cramps" as he wiped-out everyone in checkers-- and how fortunate we all were that he was the "caretaker" of our "tennis asylum." ☺

From 1953 'til now the BGTC has meant many things to many people. To capture the essence of what it was like in those "early years" is no easy task for sure. Let's just say that if you were one of those fortunate to have shared those BGTC "moments," no explanation is necessary; and if you were not, no explanation really suffices. For me personally, the BGTC was where I arrived as one who "played tennis," and where I was taught how to become a "tennis player."

When I received Dan Magill's letter re: the celebration of the 50th. Anniversary of the BGTC, immediately I began to think back, reflect on the early '60s when I first visited the Center. This was where all of the best players played. It was the "only game in town," so to speak. Other than the private social clubs, there were very few tennis facilities at that time…no Dekalb TC, no Blackburn TC, no North Fulton TC, etc…and even the best players from the social clubs would congregate at the BGTC. In fact, though it was one of the finest public facilities in the country, it had its own "club" atmosphere that made it special.

--I remember the first time I played at the Center on court 12 being introduced to all 7,200 square feet of the court by Larry Shippey (…and I thought I could play.) ☺…

--I remember Jack Rodgers, an excellent Pro and player, and how he helped me get started in tennis…

--I remember spending endless hours sitting on the bleachers by court 1 observing (i.e. "soaking it all up like a sponge") those marvelous "old Seniors," (a phrase used with the greatest of respect and admiration), and how they displayed their racket skills, athletic talents, expertise, and "smarts" there on a daily basis: Bitsy Grant, Larry Shippey, Tom Bird, Hank Crawford, Coach Dodd, "Foots" Dudley, Vince Connerat, Nat Collins, Red Enloe, to mention a few. These "old Seniors" were simply THE BEST here and in the South, and among THE BEST in the country as the National Championships they captured would attest to…and how they made the infamous "LOB" such a strategic, effective shot, and how when a match was over, oft-times their opponents needed a "'LOB'otomy" as those "MASTERS" had used that masterful shot to totally demoralize them.

--I remember the "mix" of people from the CEO to the ordinary worker; from the rich to the not-so-rich…from the very "top" tennis players to those with "delusions of adequacy" ☺; all with the common bond of the love of tennis, having fun and competition, and sharing a camaraderie/friendly atmosphere, (except where "line calls" were concerned, ☺) both on and off the court unlike anything experienced anywhere else…for once you walked through the gates to the Center, everyone was the same. There was a "connection" among the various participants that served as a "magnet" that drew everyone back to the BGTC again and again. You see, the BGTC was more than the 13 clay courts and 4 hard courts back then; more than the bleachers alongside court 1 and behind court 2; more than the clubhouse and locker rooms…yes, much, much more…The BGTC had its own PERSONALITY, which was a combination of all of the personalities that frequented the place… personalities like: "Worst-in-the-World," "Orange Bowl Champion," "Mountain Man," "Dog," "Commissioner," "Ralph-O," "Midnight," "Junior," "Doc," "Long O," "Sherlock," "Three Hundred," "Beep-Beep," "Strokes," "Turbo," "Tree," "Slow Foot," "Peanut Man," "Who Two," "The Wall," "Lefty," "The Judge," "Animal," "Teddy Bear," "World's Greatest Cardiologist,"

-2-

"Cockroach," "Pinky," "Horshack," "Chu-Chu," "White Child," "Sudsy," "Brother," "Tooth Fairy,
" "Little Gnome," "Big Coach," "199," "Newspaper Jim," "Spider," "Coyote," "Ursula," "Doc,"
"The Fun Man," "Piano Legs," "Gooey," and "Daddy."
—Where but the BGTC could you have a "Tree Club" with its regular members, Stan, Ralph, S.M.,
Sonny, Max, Danny, Jim, Nan, Harris, Andy, Lee, etc?
—I remember Carrie Howell and that "ubiquitous" glass of tea of hers, as she meandered from court
to court watching one of "hers," Speed, Richard, Peter, Jimbo, Eleanor, or Lindy, as well as others
performing--what a "classy lady!"...
—I remember the top Women players, Carol and Dana Lenahan, Mary Ann Connerat, Leigh
Frohsin, one of the smartest/most talented, and Sally Seebeck and Betty Jo Braselton the best
Women's Open Doubles team in that era...the BGTC "regulars," Eleanor Swann, Beverly Shields,
Ann James, Ruth Lay, Natalie Cohen, Louise Fowler, Margie Healey, Cooie Orr, Hope Moore,
Barbara Parr, Barbara Tregellas, Missy Payne, Mary Ann Yopp to name a few, and how they played
such a smart game of tennis..."L☺BS" anyone? ☺...
—I remember sitting on the bleachers beside court 1 and watching John Skogstad make the tennis
ball "talk," and he and Harry Thompson demolish all opponents...Wally Johnson use his serve to
crush his opponents...Bob Nichols drive his opponents "batty" with his "super-steady" game and
"pin-point" passing shots...Richard Howell and Bill Shippey defeat all comers in doubles in the
Juniors and most of the men...Crawford Henry, his tremendous serve and marvelous array of shot-
making...Allen Morris and his classic backhand...Ned and Mike Neely stand at the service line
across the net from each other and pummel the ball at ludicrous speed with seemingly endless
rallies..."Bitsy" Grant, himself, nothing short of a "magnificent maestro" with the tennis racket as
he had most players stepping on their own feet...Tom Bird and "Big Bertha," his awesome
forehand...Hank Crawford, with his 18 ounce (that's right, 18 ounces) racket, and how he held the
racket still and the ball just seemed to "propel" off of it...Larry Shippey and his "cerebral" selection
of shots, so well-executed...Ruth Lay and her talented Juniors, especially the top duo of Nancy
Yeargin and Wendy White, who went on to excel on the national scene on the Women's
Tour...Natalie Cohen, who could be seen during tournament time, all decked out in her Umpire's
blazer, and how professionally and expertly she directed those matches... Charlie Hartridge and
Davis Rives, battling each other in singles (into their 70s) each weekend at 8:00 a.m. on court 1...
—I remember, perhaps the "signature moment" of those BGTC "early years," which involved Ralph
and "Bitsy" himself. One Spring Saturday afternoon everyone was gathered around the TV set at the
bottom of the stairs outside the old Pro Shop, about 20-25 of us, as "Bitsy" came in and started down
the stairs. The Kentucky Derby was about to begin, and Ralph yelled to "Bitsy," "'Bits,' I'll take the
#4 horse against the field," whereupon Bitsy scoffed at Ralph, something like, "you can't be serious!"
Ralph replied, "Yes I am—I got an 'inside tip' from the jockey. What's the matter--you scared?"
Bitsy mumbled something and said, "you're on for 'five!'" ($5.00) About that time, the gates sprung
open and the race was on. Everything was bunched up as the horses rounded the first turn, but in the
backstretch you could see the #4 horse moving up in the pack, and as they rounded the final turn, the
#4 horse pulled even with the field, and "down the stretch," edged ahead, sure enough winning by a
couple of lengths. Ralph just laughed, and held out his hand; and Bitsy mumbled something as he
handed Ralph the five dollars. Such was the craziness at the BGTC...tennis, checkers, bridge, the
Kentucky Derby, you name it, along with a cast of characters and personalities that would challenge
any Hollywood script. There was something going on all the time either on the courts or off. Oh,
almost forgot, I don't know to this day if "Bitsy" ever found out that what we had just seen on the
TV that Saturday afternoon was an "INSTANT REPLAY" of the running of the Kentucky Derby!"
(Honest! The race had already been run, and yes, the #4 horse won that one too.) ☺ Leave it to
Ralph!
—In summary, in essence the BGTC was and is all about PE☺PLE...PE☺PLE of all backgrounds, all
sizes, all shapes, all ages, all descriptions, all levels, coming together for times of enjoyment, fun,
competition, and camaraderie. The memories of all of the "paths that chanced to cross" at the BGTC,
the memories of those unbelievable BGTC "moments," the memories of so many "special people"...I
wear all of those memories around my neck like a "rainbow," and will cherish them always.

♥"HAPPY 5☺th." BGTC!♥

ITA Collegiate Tennis Hall of Fame

Photo by the author

The Intercollegiate Tennis Association (ITA) selected the University of Georgia as the site of its Collegiate Tennis Hall of Fame in 1982. After retiring from the University of Georgia in 1995, Dan Magill serves as chairman of the Hall of Fame Committee and curator of the Hall of Fame's museum.

In 1983, the first members of the Hall of Fame were selected and enshrined in ceremonies during the NCAA Championships in Athens. Thanks to the generosity of the Rogers family (Athenian Marianne and famous singer Kenny), the Hall of Fame building was dedicated during the 1984 NCAAs. The Hall of Fame inducts members annually, honoring past collegiate players, coaches and contributors dating back to 1883 when the first national tournament was held, making tennis the oldest national collegiate championship.

Visitors to the Hall of Fame can view more than 800 photographs and murals, featuring Hall of Fame members, NCAA singles, doubles and team champions, winners of ITA's national tournaments, collegians who have excelled in Davis Cup play and Grand Slam winners. There are numerous racquets used by champions from different eras, including those used by the first U.S. Davis Cup team players in 1900, and the first tennis rulebook in the country (1879).

Private donations fund the Hall of Fame operations including the upkeep and improvement of the numerous displays. Contributions to assist in the development of the Hall of Fame are tax deductible. Checks should be made payable to ITA Hall of Fame and sent to the attention of the Curator, Tennis Hall of Fame, P.O. Box 1472, Athens, GA 30603.

The museum houses not only collegiate tennis memorabilia but hundreds of pictures of famous tennis players in the state of Georgia, and displays full size news clippings of tournaments and tennis events over the last century. A few are displayed here, courtesy of Dan Magill.

In 1900, the U S won the first Davis Cup Match, against Great Britain, at the Longwood Cricket Club in Boston. L to R are Malcom Whitman, Harvard 1899, NCAA singles winner in 1896; Dwight Davis, Harvard 1900, NCAA singles and doubles champion, 1899; and Holcomb Ward, Harvard 1900, NCAA doubles champion 1899.

Joseph S. Clark of Philadelphia, right, was the first collegiate champion, winning the "intercollegiates" singles and doubles in Hartford, CN in 1883. He won the U.S. doubles championship with Richard Sears, Harvard, at Newport, RI in 1895. He was president of the United States Lawn Tennis Association from 1889 through 1891, and is a member of the International Tennis Hall of Fame.

Above, the 1928 UGA team, L-R Joe Boland, Malon Courts, Bill Legwen, and Hamilton Napier.

Left, University of Georgia's 1911 tennis team, L-R Tom Brand, Dewalt Cohen, Frank Carter (Captain), R.E. Lanham, and Richard Goodwyr.

Above, John Beavers, UGA, '31, '32, and '33, with his trophies, most of which were won playing doubles with Wilmer Hines. In the summer of 1930 they won the NC State and SC State Championships, the Cotton States, the Tri-State in Memphis, the Southern Open, the Western Carolina, the Kentucky State, the USTA Boys' 18's, and the Southern Juniors.

L. A. Cothran, left, of Greenville, SC, played for the University of Georgia and won the "Patterson Cup" in 1897, and "intercollegiate championship" in 1898. He graduated from Atlanta's Boys High while living with his brother-in-law, John Graves. The two, helped by Henry Thornton, Nat's older brother, built a crude dirt court near their home in College Park to practice on.

Above, UGA players L.B. Lee and H. H. Deane won the 1906 NCAA doubles.

Doubles partners and roommates Manuel Diaz, left, now Mens Tennis Coach, University of Georgia, and Gordon Smith, now CEO of the United States Tennis Association; in 1972.

GEORGIA'S GORDON SMITH NAMED COMMANDER-IN-CHIEF OF USTA

Congratulations to former Georgia tennis star Gordon Smith who has been named "commander-in-chief" of the United States Tennis Association.

In November he will succeed Lee Hamilton as executive director and chief operating officer of the USTA, who has retired after a five-year distinguished career.

The USTA is the national governing body for the sport of tennis in the U.S. and the leader in promoting and developing the growth of tennis at every level -- from local communities to the highest level of the professional game. It owns and operates the US Open, the largest annually attended sporting event in the world, and launched the US Open Series linking 10 summer tournaments to the US Open. In addition, it owns the 94 Pro Circuit events throughout the U.S., and selects the teams for the Davis Cup, Fed Cup, Olympic and Paralympic Games. A not-for-profit organization with 700,000 members, it invests 100% of its proceeds in growing the game.

Smith was a star on four straight SEC championship teams at Georgia in 1972-3-4-5.

His four-year roommate in college was Manuel Diaz. They formed one of the strongest doubles teams in the nation: the 6-3 Diaz (a right-hander with a big top-spin serve) and Smith (a southpaw with a slashing, slice serve). They won the SEC, Southern Collegiate, Princeton Indoors — and also won four matches in the 1975 NCAAs at Corpus Christi reaching the quarter-finals but had to default when Diaz went to the hospital with heat prostration.

Both have continued to excel in their chosen professions. Diaz has guided Georgia to three NCAA team titles (1999, 2001, and 2007) as well as five runner-up finishes.

Smith also chose a "court" career. He has been with the South's most prestigious international law firm, King and Spalding since 1980, specializing in trial work and litigation. He has been listed in the publication *The Best Lawyers in America* for many years.

It was quite an honor for him to be his firm's main spokesman when one of their biggest clients, Williamson Tobacco Company (makers of Lucky Strike cigarettes, etc.) was in the public eye in 1994. Many readers will recall Mike Wallace of the celebrated 60 Minutes TV Show debating Gordon Smith on tobacco issues. Gordon more than held his own with the intimidating Wallace.

Smith does volunteer work with the State Bar of Georgia and American Bar Association in which capacity he was lured back into his first love: tennis. His college contemporary John Callen, at Georgia Tech, then executive secretary of the Southern Tennis Assn., asked him to be the general counsel for the STA. And, through the years Smith has been a member of the STA Board of Directors and executive vice-president of the STA, which led to important positions with the USTA: Adult and Senior Competition Committee, Constitution and Rules Committee (Chairman), Grievance Committee (Vice-Chairman) and, Vice-President, USTA.

1983 NCAA doubles winners Ola Malmqvist (far left) and Allen Miller (far right) celebrate with Coaches Dan Magill (foreground) and Manny Diaz.

In 1941, the University of Georgia tennis courts were behind LeConte Hall. Court caretaker Dan Magill, far right, with Albert Boykin, later to become UGA's tennis coach, and "Hambone" Johnson.

For many years, a highlight of the NCAA finals tournament, when held in Athens, Georgia, was the Paris Island Marine Band's performance during the opening ceremonies, arranged by WWII Marine Major Dan Magill

Right, in the 1952 Crackerland open singles, Georgia Tech star Frank Willett, right, defeated Allen Morris (later to star on the Presbyterian College team and reach the quarters of Wimbledon a few years later).

Left, in the 1953 singles, Bill Umsteader, right, defeated Donald Floyd

Left, In the 1959 Crackerland singles (left), Georgia Tech star Bob Nichols (far right) defeated UGA star Lindsey Hopkins III in the singles final.

Right, in the open doubles, oldsters Bitsy Grant and Bobby Dodd, prevailed over Vince Connerat (far left) and Dr. Glenn Dudley

Right, 1953 Crackerland Veteran's division singles winner Davis Rives, far left, next to singles runner up (and doubles partner) Guy Rainey and their doubles runner up opponents W.W. Davidson and Dr. Robert West.

Allen Miller, 1987, above and right,
enroute to winning the Atlanta City Singles

Bitsy Grant and former UGA star Mikael Pernfors as partners
in the Celebrity Doubles, 1984 NCAA finals, Athens, Georgia

Dan Magill's tribute to Lindsey Hopkins III

The Georgia tennis family mourns the death of Lindsey Hopkins III, who on Saturday lost a month-long battle to pulmonary fibrosis in Atlanta's Piedmont hospital. It will long remember and appreciate the major contributions he made to his alma mater.I first met Lindsey in the early 1950s in his first appearance at the Crackerland junior tournament on Georgia's varsity courts. He was the ace of the renowned professional Jack Waters' star-studded Piedmont Driving Club group that annually dominated the Crackerland.

That's also when I first met Lindsey's famous father, Lindsey Hopkins Jr., the No. 2 Coca-Cola stockholder (behind Bob Woodruff) and the man considered by many as the top sportsman in the country. He was a mainstay at the Indianapolis 500, sometimes entering two cars. He had been the chairman of the first Southern Junior Davis Cup committee in the early 1930s, at which time he also brought the first tennis teaching pro to the Piedmont Driving Club.

When I became Georgia's tennis coach in 1955, we didn't have any scholarships, but most of the best young players in the state were protégés of Jack Waters and sons of UGA alumni. They didn't need scholarships. So, in 1956 I asked the parents of three outstanding juniors (Lindsey Hopkins III, Richard Courts II and Alfred Thompson Jr.) to send their sons to their alma mater. That's how we recruited the best freshman team in Georgia history (at that time).

Lindsey III twice won the State Collegiate singles (1956 and 1959) and doubles (1956 and 1957) with Alfred Thompson. He and Thompson won the Eastern Intercollegiate freshman doubles in 1956. Lindsey and Harry Thompson (Georgia Tech) twice won the tough Crackerland men's doubles (1958 and 1959) and Lindsey captained Georgia's team, which finished third in the 1959 SEC tournament. Lindsey was a superb volleyer. In fact, the Lindsey Hopkins Volleying Award is given each year to the Georgia player most proficient with that shot.

In 1972 Georgia held the NCAA championships for the first time. Five years later (1977) the NCAA said it wanted Georgia to be the semi-permanent site of its men's championships. So, athletic director Joel Eaves built a stadium seating more than 3,000 fans. We also needed indoor courts so that matches could be played there during inclement weather. I asked young Lindsey if his dad would finance the construction costs, and he took me to see his dad at his office in Buckhead. Big Lindsey gladly agreed to build the indoor courts, and they were dedicated with the SEC Indoor championships in January 1980 - and Georgia triumphed.

The Lindsey Hopkins Indoor courts have been the biggest factor in Georgia becoming a national power in tennis. They have enabled the team to practice every day, regardless of weather, and they have helped to recruit top players to Georgia.

Young Lindsey Hopkins had some big shoes to fill when his father died Feb. 14, 1986. Atlanta sports editors Furman Bisher (Journal) and Jesse Outlar (Constitution) paid their highest tributes to him. Bisher's column was entitled 'A Priceless Sportsman' and concluded with these lines: "Rich he was, but the wealth you saw of him in sports was his jovial nature and good fellowship. There is no price to be put on that."

Outlar penned, "He was one of the last of a vanishing breed of true sportsmen, a raconteur and as fine a gentleman as I've met in sports or any other profession. A graduate of UGA's Terry College of Business Administration, Lindsey III in 1991 received the Distinguished Alumnus Award. He served as president of the Terry College Alumni Board of Directors, and has been most generous in his financial support of the Terry College and the tennis program. His countless friends and old teammates will overflow Trinity Presbyterian Church at his funeral services at 11 a.m. Thursday.

Lindsey's last act before he entered the hospital, was to finalize plans for he and his family (wife Wanda, daughters and their husbands), to be with him in Indianapolis May 21 for the induction of his father in the Indianapolis 500 Hal of Fame. His family still plans to be there. Lindsey and his father will, too.

Dan Magill, 2004

EPILOGUE

ASTONISHED

That's how the players in the first 50 or so pages of this book would feel if they had heard somebody talk about how kids under 15 were going to start quitting school to play tennis for money. There was no "money" out there, and you learned to play tennis by watching someone else play, and you got a few tips from good players. The game was about competition and tournaments, not about money.

Now they're doing just that. Search "tennis academies Atlanta" on your computer, and you get dozens of them. "School" for a couple of hours in the morning, then toss the books aside and hit balls, balls, and more balls, and then start playing entry level pro events. A lot of parents start their kids on this path, in spite of the overwhelming odds against ever making a living "playing tennis for money."

It's a perplexing fascination. Bo Hodge, a talented young junior player from Athens, Georgia, spent his last two high school years in Boca Raton, FL, training with Andy Roddick, Mardy Fish, and David Martin, being coached by South African Pro Sanford Boster. The four of them lived in the Boster home, and attended classes at "Boca Prep." When he started playing Futures and Challenger events, he said it was like "...hitting the wall." He played all over the world, but ultimately decided to pass up a pro playing career, and UGA was delighted to give him a full scholarship. He didn't disappoint; All American honors four straight years, and now assistant tennis coach at Alabama.

UGA star John Isner: *"I never even thought about going pro after high school...if I hadn't gone to college, I really don't even know if I would be playing tennis now. A lot of players leave high school and go straight to the pros, and they (some) don't make it and burn out after two or three years.*

College was the best preparation I could have ever asked for... in those four years at Georgia I had unbelievable coaching from Coach Diaz. I learned so much mentally, and I got so much stronger physically. Coming out of high school I was tall, skinny and gangly, not strong and not mature...I had to go to college and get stronger. I had to start growing out instead of up."

Is "Monday Night Tennis" imminent? Not likely. "World Team Tennis," starting in the '70's, has had a checkered run, still surviving but never reaching the popularity of other major spectator sports, and it's DOA now in Georgia. The "Atlanta Thunder" boasted Martina Navratilova and Larry Stefanki. When they won the league, '91 and '92, no one seemed to care, and then it fizzled. That first year, they played at Dekaib Tennis Center, hardly a world class venue, then at WCT, but fans just did not support it.

A lot of people like to play tennis, but when it comes to watching, most of them want to see physical stuff, some hits, somebody getting "decked" or "trucked" (*Oh, did his helmet fly off? He's not moving*); 300 pound linesmen plowing through opponents like a runaway Peterbilt, some "lumber in the teeth," a trickle of blood at the corner of somebody's mouth (never mind that by some estimates 75% of the participants in pro boxing have criminal records). "Extreme Cage Fighting" features a "guillotine choke", and fighters flip off the audience. Video clips of "Best football hits" are popular on the internet. Concussions, cheap shots, and quarterbacks getting sacked, hammered, and carried off the field seem to sell ads.

C'est la vie.

INDEX

INDEX